942.05

A HISTORY OF BRITAIN

BOOK III

This third volume of the evolving series covers the Tudor period (1485-1603), widely seen as the 'golden age' of England's maturing into nationhood. A cohesive sense of identity and pervading spirit of discovery brought down the curtain on the Middle Ages and raised it on the Renaissance...and Reformation, with Henry VIII breaking with Rome's papacy. Columbus' crossing the Atlantic (1492) would lead English sailors (like Drake) to venture to the New World and beyond. Queen Elizabeth Ist's fleet was to defeat mighty Spain's Armada in 1588, while England's Marlowe, Shakespeare and composers set new standards in creative arts.

EH Carter was Chief Inspector of Schools in the 1930s and '40s.
RAF Mears taught history at Warwick School between 1923 and 1933.

David Evans, who edits the restored series, is an historian and former Head of History at Eton College.

PUBLICATION SCHEDULE

A HISTORY OF BRITAIN

BOOK III

The Tudors ♦ 1485-1603

by

EH Carter & RAF Mears

edited and updated by

David Evans

A History of Britain
Book III

STACEY INTERNATIONAL
128 Kensington Church Street
London W8 4BH
Tel: +44 (0)20 7221 7166; Fax: +44 (0)20 7792 9288
Email: info@stacey-international.co.uk
www.stacey-international.co.uk

ISBN: 978 1906768 22 5

Original edition published in 1937 by The Clarendon Press

1 3 5 7 9 0 8 6 4 2

Printed in the UAE

The Publishers of this edition of *The History of Britain*, revised by David Evans
(formerly Head of History, Eton College), give wholehearted acknowledgment to the
original work of the late E H Carter (sometime Chief Examiner in History, Board of
Education, and H M Inspector of Schools) and R A F Mears (former Senior History
Master, Warwick School), who died respectively in 1954 and 1940. The Publishers
declare that prolonged endeavours devoted to tracing whether rights to the work of
these two distinguished scholars rested with any successors or assigns have been
without avail, and that they remain ready to indemnify, as may be mutually deemed
appropriate, proven holders of such rights.

Cover image courtesy of FCIT

CIP Data: A catalogue record for this book is available from the British Library

Contents

List of Illustrations

List of Maps

OUTLINE SUMMARY

TUDOR PERIOD (1485-1603)

BRITISH ISLES	ABROAD
1485 Henry VII acc.	1492 Columbus (America)
	1498 Vasco da Gama (India)
1509-47 Henry VIII	1517 Luther's Theses
1515 Wolsey Chancellor	
1529-36 Reformation Parliament	1519-56 Emperor Charles V
	1534 Cartier (Canada)
1535-39 Dissolution of Monasteries	
	1541 Calvin at Geneva
1549 First Prayer Book (Edward VI)	
1554 Mary I marries Philip of Spain	
1558-1603 Elizabeth	1562 Hawkins – Slave Trade
1559 Acts of Supremacy and Uniformity	
	1577-80 Drake round the World
	1583 Gilbert (Newfoundlandland)
1587 Mary Queen of Scots executed	
1588 Spanish Armada	
	1600 East India Company

THE AGE OF THE RENAISSANCE:
INTRODUCTION

THE Renaissance was a change in Europeans' way of understanding the world which took place during the centuries from the fourteenth to the sixteenth. Renaissance is in origin a French word that means rebirth. The term is used because central to the change was a revival of interest in the learning of ancient Greece and Rome, which had enormous effects on the arts and literature of modern Europeans.

But why was the renewed study of Greek learning of vital importance in the history of Europe? The Greek view of life was, in many respects, the opposite to the medieval. The Church in the Middle Ages had taught men to revere authority and to find in its teaching an answer to all the problems of life, whereas the Greeks taught men to inquire and to explore rather than to accept. They advocated enjoyment of physical beauty in this life rather than denial of earthly pleasure for the sake of bliss in the life to come in heaven. It was this attitude of mind, more than anything else, which shook the medieval world to its foundations. Some leading Renaissance thinkers even began to scorn the Middle Ages as a time of cultural darkness, unmindful of the fact that, narrow as the medieval culture was in some respects, yet it gave much to the world that has never been surpassed, and that the work of the Renaissance itself was partly made possible by the achievements of the great medieval centuries.

The Renaissance brought many changes: it deeply influenced learning and education, art and architecture; science was transformed and inventions were made, exploration revolutionized the understanding of geography, and religion altered fundamentally. We will consider in turn each of these aspects.

After the fall of Rome, a knowledge of Greek had rapidly died out in the West and no provision was made for its teaching similar to that made for Latin. In Italy, owing to the closeness of its relations with the East, the number of scholars, monks, and others, who learnt some Greek was greater than elsewhere. It is not surprising, therefore, that the revival of learning received its main impulse from Italy. From the

The Revival of Learning time (c. 1350) of Petrarch and Boccaccio, Italian scholars became more and more devoted to ancient studies, and some began to visit Constantinople, where Greek learning had been preserved. There they hunted out, copied, and eagerly studied the precious manuscripts of the past, and these opened up a new world of thought. Further, from the time after 1350 when the Turks began to make conquests in Europe, some of the Greeks themselves began to travel westwards and to accept well-paid teaching posts in the wealthy Italian cities. And, though the revival began in Italy, the new ideas were rapidly circulated by the new printing presses, and every nation of western Europe in due course played its part in the Renaissance.

The great and wealthy city of Florence was the first centre of the Italian Renaissance. Cosimo de Medici, a merchant prince who

Florence became ruler of the city (1434-64), was a patron of the New Learning, and he encouraged Greek scholars to settle in Florence. His grandson, Lorenzo de Medici (ruled 1469-92), known as The Magnificent, loved to gather round him the learned men of the day; he spent £60,000 a year on books; and he caused 200 rare manuscripts to be brought from the East to the Medici library.

By 1500 Rome had become the most important centre of the New Learning. The Popes themselves became great patrons of learning. Nicholas V (1447-55) founded the Vatican Library, one of the greatest in the world. When the son of Lorenzo de Medici became

Rome Pope as Leo X (1513-21), the Renaissance in Rome reached its highest point. Leo made Rome, as he said, 'the capital of the world in literature, as it is in everything else'. He provided a hundred professors for his Greek college in Rome, and he brought his father's library to the Holy City. The library was afterwards restored to Florence (where it still is) by his cousin Clement VII (Pope 1523-34), another member of this remarkable Medici family.

Fortunately, the improved manufacture of paper and the invention of printing by movable type coincided with the Revival of Learning. Movable type was made in Germany by Gutenberg of Mainz, and it was he who printed the Letter of Indulgence granted by Pope Nicholas V in aid of funds for a Crusade against the Turks, which bears the earliest (European) printed date (1453). A generation later in 1476 William Caxton introduced the printing press into England. At the end of the fifteenth century a beautiful type, known as the Italic, was invented by the printer, Aldo Manuzio (1450-1515), who set up the famous Aldine Press at Venice.

Printing

The New Learning influenced England from the time of Edward IV, and it made great headway in the reigns of Henry VII and Henry VIII, when it flourished particularly at Oxford. The first

The New Learning in England

THE INVENTION OF PRINTING
The interior of a printing press in the 16th century. Notice the compositors sitting in front of their cases of type, with the author's manuscript pinned up above; the man coming in at the door with a supply of paper; and the two presses, at one of which the workman is inking the type, and at the other a sheet is being printed.

Englishman to bring Greek manuscripts to England was William Selling (c. 1465), a Fellow of All Souls, Oxford, and a teacher at Christ Church School, Canterbury. One of his pupils was Thomas Linacre, who went to Florence and shared the instruction given to the young Medici princes; he read in the Vatican Library, and made the acquaintance of Aldo at Venice. Like all the great men of the Renaissance, Linacre was interested in all branches of knowledge, including medicine. He was King's Physician to Henry VII and Henry VIII, and he helped to found in London the Royal College of Physicians (1518). Another Oxford teacher who drew his inspiration from Italian sources was William Grocyn, one of the first men to give lectures on Greek literature at his University. One of Grocyn's pupils was John Colet, who visited Italy (1496) and returned to lecture on the Gospels (in the Greek original) at Oxford. Colet re-founded St. Paul's School, London (1510). He and Sir Thomas More, another man of great learning and piety, were friends of Erasmus, a Dutch scholar of international fame. Lady Margaret Beaufort, mother of Henry VII, was herself a patroness of the New Learning. She founded two Cambridge colleges, Christ's and St. John's, and two (still flourishing) Lady Margaret Professorships of Divinity, one at Oxford and one at Cambridge.

The Revival of Learning was one aspect of the Renaissance; the wonderful outburst of artistic energy in the fifteenth and sixteenth centuries was another. The painters of the new period broke away from the artistic traditions of the Middle Ages and sought to create pictures which might almost deceive the viewer into supposing that he was looking at a view through a window, as they believed ancient artists had done. Sculptors such as Donatello (1386-1466) aimed to make their statues look as if they could move and express emotion. The great figures of that age – Botticelli, Leonardo da Vinci, Michelangelo, Raphael, Titian – still loom large in the history of European art. Examples of their works, and of many other Italian artists of the Renaissance, as well as of the Northern artists such as

Painting and sculpture

Holbein and Dürer are to be seen in the magnificent collection at the
National Gallery.

It was natural that men who sought their inspiration from the
Greeks and Romans should turn with renewed interest to classical   Architecture
architecture. The ruins of ancient Rome provided examples ready
to hand; and soon churches planned like classical temples were rising
in many Italian cities. In Rome, for example, Old St. Peter's
was pulled down and replaced by a new cathedral which borrowed
many features from ancient architecture. Bramante made the original
plan and the famous dome was added later by Michelangelo.
Renaissance architecture did not fully establish itself in England till
the end of the reign of Queen Elizabeth, though Henry VII's tomb
at Westminster Abbey is an example of the Florentine art of the
period.

The Renaissance period, filled as it was with a love of experiment,
naturally produced a renewed interest in science. In the Middle Ages
the scientific theories of the ancients were known and commented   Science
on. In the Renaissance period, however, there was a new spirit of
inquiry and experiment, which is best illustrated from the life of
Leonardo da Vinci (1452-1519). Like so many of the great men of
that age, Leonardo was a Florentine. Not only was he a painter,
sculptor, and architect of great merit; he was also a highly original
thinker and a designer of scientific appliances.[1] A letter which he   Leonardo
wrote to the Duke of Milan, asking for employment, is very   da Vinci
illuminating. The first nine sections of the letter concern the use of
scientific inventions in war – a sad forecast of the uses to which
science was to be put in the future. Only when he arrives at the tenth
section the author says: 'In times of peace, I believe I can compete

---

[1] His note-books have been found to contain valuable ideas in physics, dynamics,
and other branches of science. For long they puzzled the students of manuscripts,
and small wonder, for he used his own 'shorthand', wrote from right to left, and
omitted the use of punctuation.

with anyone in architecture, in the construction of public and private monuments and in the building of canals. I am able to execute statues in marble, bronze and clay; in painting I can do as well as anyone else.' Here was a truly remarkable man. Modern Science begins its history with the Renaissance and owes a good deal to Leonardo's fertile brain. He was the first of a long line of experimenters whose work has continued to the present day.

The greatest shock to the medieval notions of the universe was

Copernicus given by a learned Polish canon, Copernicus. For two thousand years mankind with few exceptions had believed that the earth was the centre of the universe, and that the sun revolved round our planet every twenty-four hours. Such had been the teaching of Ptolemy, the Greek scientist. Another Greek, Pythagoras, had questioned it, and advanced the extraordinary notion that the sun, not the earth, was the centre of the universe; but there were few who accepted his theory until Copernicus turned his attention to the 'solar system'. Just before he died in 1543 he published a book, *The Revolutions of the Heavenly Bodies*, in which he argued that Pythagoras' sun-centred universe made better sense of all the observations of the movements of the planets than did Ptolemy's theory. Twenty years later the famous Galileo was born at Pisa, and it was he who perfected the telescope (a Dutch invention of 1609). He lived to popularize the theory of Copernicus, but he was nearly put to death for his pains and was forced by the Court of Inquisition to recant. The Italian Galileo, and the Englishman Newton, who showed that the same laws of motion which explained movement on earth also explained the movements of the heavenly bodies, were the two greatest scientists of the seventeenth century.[2]

The New   In the realm of geographical discovery, no age in the world's
World history was more momentous than the Age of the Renaissance.

---

[2] For the first important age of science in England – the seventeenth century – see Book IV, Chapter VI.

Columbus, who discovered America; Vasco da Gama, who found the Cape Route to India; Cabot, Cartier, and Cortes, the discoverers of Newfoundland, Canada, and Mexico; Balboa, who first sailed on the Pacific; Magellan, whose ship was the first to sail round the world – all these and many more make the fifteenth and sixteenth centuries an era without parallel in the annals of discovery.

The new ideas which came surging into the world during the Renaissance acted in many respects as disruptive forces. This was particularly true in the realm of religion. The revival of Greek learning was bound to have an effect on religion, since Greek is the original language of the New Testament. The teaching of the 16th century Church was challenged by new interpretations of the message of the Bible. People could also compare the moral state of the Church and Papacy of their own time with the state of the early Church described in the New Testament, and voices were raised demanding reforms. Some reformers, like Colet and Erasmus, tried to reconcile the new ideas with the Church of Rome and worked to reform it; others, of whom Luther was the greatest, rejected altogether its authority. The revolution in European history known as the Reformation was partly an indirect result of the Renaissance – of the New Learning which invited comparison between the present and the past; of the invention of printing which broadcast the new ideas; and again, of the growing idea of the supremacy of the State.

Religious change

I

Trade and Discovery

1. East and West

THE best way to understand the limitations of the medieval notions of the world is to look at a medieval map. There is one, of the thirteenth century, preserved in Hereford Cathedral – a round world drawn on a flat board. The land-mass is divided into the three continents of Asia, Europe, and Africa, and in the centre is Jerusalem. All round the outside edge runs the ocean – the farther limits of which were unknown. In this map the largest and most important sea is the Mediterranean, connecting the three continents of the Old World. The Red Sea and the Persian Gulf lead away to the Indies, vaguely known beyond. The British Isles therefore lay on the extreme edge of the medieval world; our ancestors sailed their ships eastwards to the Continent, not westwards into the unknown Atlantic.

However, the barren Atlantic coast of the Sahara was well known to the Moors, who were masters of North Africa, and some time in the Middle Ages they discovered the Guinea coast. Somewhere on that coast was supposed to exist 'Bilad Ghana' or the 'Land of Wealth'. From this land the Christian traders of Europe were excluded by Moorish jealousy – but it was still possible to reach it by sea. Thus the Age of Discovery began, in the Middle Ages, with the coasting of the Atlantic shore of the Sahara first by the Genoese and then by the Portuguese, and with the latter's slave-raiding expeditions down the Guinea coast.

Portuguese Discoveries

By the fifteenth century, Portugal, situated (like England) on the edge of the known world, had taken the lead in maritime exploration under the direction of Prince Henry, grandson of John of Gaunt and later known as 'the Navigator'. Prince Henry took for his model the saintly Crusader and King of France of two centuries earlier, 'my lord

16

St. Louis' (as he calls him in his will), for Henry, like St. Louis, was inspired with the prospect of converting the heathen of Africa to the Gospel. The Age of Discovery owed much to the influence of Roman Christianity; the spread of the Gospel – sometimes by forcible means – went hand in hand with discovery.

In due course the sailors of Portugal even ventured out into the Atlantic Ocean, which was at this time regarded with dread by European sailors. Some of the Azores and the Canaries had, however, already been discovered (fourteenth century); and among Prince Henry's earliest triumphs was the finding, by one of his mariners, of Madeira (1420). Each new point reached was a triumph for the keen watcher at Sagres (near Cape St. Vincent), where he had built an observatory and a school for navigators. His thoughts were then directed towards the gold – and slave-producing coasts of Guinea. In 1441 his sailors reached Cape Blanco, in 1445 the rivers Gambia and Senegal, and in 1446 the Cape Verde Islands. In 1460 Henry died, just before his sailors reached the Gulf of Guinea and opened up a rich trade in ivory, gold, and slaves. Then, for the next twenty-seven years (1460-87) Portuguese sailors searched for a sea passage to the East. At last Bartholomew Diaz was blown round the Cape of Storms Diaz (1487), which his king renamed the Cape of Good Hope – the hope of opening trade with the Indies. Five years later three ships sailed from Spain on an even more momentous voyage.

Christopher Columbus was a Genoese sailor who had been from Columbus his youth in the Portuguese maritime service, had married a Portuguese wife, and had often been employed in the Guinea voyages; and he had sailed to Britain and even Iceland. For eighteen years he tried to persuade the rulers of Portugal and Spain to furnish him with ships for a voyage into the Atlantic. Columbus was strongly influenced by the work of Prince Henry, whose ideals were much the same as his own. Like Prince Henry, Columbus dreamed of planting the Cross in the realm of the Great Khan of Cathay, and of converting the millions of heathen to the faith of Christ. To all this he added something of his own. He believed that he was inspired by Heaven to do a great work; and that it was his mission to cross the hitherto unexplored waters of the Atlantic. What he expected to find on the other side is something of a mystery – the man himself was something of a mystery. Perhaps he thought he would reach India – or Cathay and Zipangu (i.e. China and Japan). Perhaps – who knows? – he believed that through his agency God would reveal some fresh marvel to mankind.

It is certain that Columbus and other leading geographers of the fifteenth century believed the world to be a sphere, and that therefore China and India might be reached by sailing westward instead of labouring round Africa. In the very year of Columbus' great voyage (1492), the learned geographer Martin Behaim produced his *globe*, showing what he thought to be the distribution of land and sea in both hemispheres. A glance at the map made from this globe will reveal the fact that Behaim underestimated the distance between the Azores and Cathay. He was of course ignorant of the existence of America and of the Pacific Ocean!

Discovery
of America

After long years of waiting, Columbus at last persuaded Isabella, Queen of Castile, to furnish him with three tiny ships. He set sail (3 August 1492) from Palos, near Cadiz, with a crew of 88 men, whose friends never expected to see them again. No words can do justice to the faith and perseverance of the great commander, without whose inspiration the crew of 'muttering shoalbrains' would never have dared to sail into the unknown. He revived their drooping spirits by making the most of such signs of land as they saw – floating rushes, land birds flying, and so on. At last, nearly five weeks after the explorers had left the Canaries, at two o'clock in the morning of 12 October 1492, a sailor on board the *Pinta* reported land in sight.

Columbus landed on one of the Bahama Islands. He thought he had reached the Indies, as the name of the 'West Indies' reminds us to this day. He returned home by a northerly route, and passed the Azores with two battered ships – the third had been wrecked. He sailed up the Tagus in March 1493.

Columbus made three more voyages across the Atlantic, but he never found the desired passage to India. He died (1506) after suffering many indignities at the hands of the Spanish authorities, for they meted out scant justice to the great man who, without knowing it, 'gave a New World to Spain', as his epitaph expressed it.

It was after Columbus returned from his second voyage of exploration (1496) that the long-desired African passage to India was discovered. Vasco da Gama, a Portuguese, following in the wake of Diaz, rounded the Cape of Good Hope, and at last reached Calicut in India (1498). A new route to the East was open.

Vasco da Gama 1497-8

2. Europe's Trade with the East

The trade with the East was in those days closely concerned with the health and comfort of the people of Europe. There were then no root crops such as turnips and swedes with which to feed the cattle in winter months; therefore most of the cattle had to be killed off every autumn, and the people lived on salted meat until the following summer. To make such food more palatable, the spices of the East seemed a necessity – cloves and nutmegs from the Moluccas, pepper and ginger from Malabar, cinnamon from Ceylon, nutmegs from Amboyna. And it must be remembered that in those days men had to do without potatoes, without tea or coffee or chocolate or tobacco. The East was the source of all kinds of luxuries – of 'precious stones and pearls, and various drugs and spices', as Marco Polo had written in the 13th century.

The Spice Isles

'Beyond the Bay of Bengal, near the Equator, there was opium, the only conqueror of pain then known; and in two small islands of the Moluccas, Ternate and Tidor, there was the clove tree, surpassing all plants in value. These were the real Spice Islands the enchanted region which was the object of such passionate desire; and their produce was so cheap on the spot, so dear in the markets of Antwerp and London, as to constitute the most lucrative trade in the world. From these exotics, grown on volcanic soil in the most generous of the tropical climates the profit was such as they could be paid for in precious metals ... When Drake was at Ternate, he found the Sultan hung with chains of bullion, and clad in a robe of gold brocade thick enough to stand upright.'[3]

Old and new routes to the East

The lure of this rich and romantic trade was one of the motives that inspired the sailor of the Renaissance period to 'entrust his frail bark to the cruel ocean'. To reach the markets of Asia by sea was the aim of all the great discoverers – da Gama, Columbus, Cabot, Magellan, and others – and on the way they found Africa and a New World. The Portuguese, we have seen, first found a sea-way to the East. With da Gama's arrival at Calicut (1498) in India, they saw that they could capture the Indian Ocean trade from the Arabs. This caused the old overland trade with the East to decline.

The great commercial towns of medieval Europe, like Venice and Genoa, eventually lost their supremacy as the new Atlantic trade-route superseded the old Mediterranean route leading to the caravan journey across Asia. The new route was less costly and risky than when rich cargoes had to be lifted from the backs of camels and pack-horses or carried in Chinese junks and Arab dhows. Incidentally, the caravan-route was made too dangerous by the Turkish advance, particularly after the conquest of Egypt by Sultan Selim I (1512-20). The European countries which benefited by the change were naturally those facing the Atlantic, first Portugal and Spain, and later, France, Holland, and England.

---

[3] Acton, *Lectures on Modern History*

3. The New World

The momentous discoveries of a new route to the Old World of the East, and of a New World in the West, changed the course of history, and marked the transition from the crusading age to the age of commerce and colonization. Further marvellous advances in man's knowledge of the world were made in the short space of forty years between the first voyage of Columbus and the discovery of Peru (1492-1532) – when books about the great discoveries were (as Sir Thomas More tells us) 'in every man's hand'.

With two exceptions, all the fruits of discovery at first went to Spain and Portugal, who reaped the advantage of having been first on the scene. To prevent disputes between the two countries, Pope Alexander VI issued a Bull (1493), amicably dividing all the newly discovered lands between Spain and Portugal. A line was drawn 100 leagues west of the Azores; all lands west of this line were to go to Spain, all east of it to Portugal.[4] It was this Bull which gave the Spaniards a religious sanction for their conquest and conversion of the New World and for their claim to monopolize its treasures – a claim which was afterwards contested by Elizabethan sailors.

Twenty years passed after Columbus' most famous voyage before the existence of the Pacific Ocean was revealed (1513). During that time the explorers who followed in his wake pushed north and south along the coasts of Central and South America in the hope of finding a passage to the East. For the results of Columbus' discovery were at first disappointing. Instead of the wealth and wonders of the East, which the Portuguese sailors had reached, the Spaniards had found only some islands and an unknown continent, peopled by brown-skinned 'Indians', some harmless, some savage, but all uncivilized. The islands were beautiful, it is true, and their beauty appealed to

Spain and Portugal

Exploration of America

---

[4] The next year, by the Treaty of Tordesillas, the line was moved farther west in Portugal's favour.

the fine nature of Columbus, who compared the birds and flowers of the West Indies with those of the gardens of Andalusia in the springtime. But the successors of Columbus cared nothing for the beauties of the West Indies; they sought wealth, and they cruelly treated the natives. Later on, the Spaniards followed the miserable practice of the Portuguese in enslaving the negroes of West Africa, whom they shipped across the Atlantic, and worked as slaves on the West Indian sugar plantations.

Meanwhile, thousands of miles of the American coastline were being opened up. The north coast of South America, from Brazil to Panama (see map, pp. 26-27), was explored by Pinzon (one of Columbus' captains) and others. A Portuguese named Cabral, who was blown out of his course to India westwards came upon the eastern coast of Brazil, which he claimed for Portugal (1500). In the following year Amerigo Vespucci, a Florentine – whose Christian name was given to the new world as America – explored the 2,000 miles of coast farther south. In 1513 Balboa, a Spanish adventurer, first sighted the Pacific Ocean from a hill in Darien (Panama) and built a ship to sail on that unknown sea. Six years later Magellan sailed in the service of the King of Spain on a wonderful voyage, which linked up all the previous discoveries. He pushed right down the coast of South America until he found the tortuous and difficult passage – the Straits of Magellan – which led at last to the Pacific Ocean. He sailed right across that huge expanse of water till he came to the East Indies, where he discovered the Philippines.[5] Magellan was killed by natives in the Philippines, but his crew brought his ship home across the Indian Ocean, round the Cape of Good Hope, back to Spain (September 1522). This ship, the *Vittoria*, was the first to sail round the world.

In the same year that Magellan started on his famous voyage Cortes landed at Vera Cruz in the Gulf of Mexico. After a few days'

Cabral

The Pacific discovered 1513

Magellan 1519-22

Cortes

---

[5] They were so named later on, after Philip II of Spain.

march inland he came upon the marvellous city of Mexico, built on an island in a lake. It was the capital of the Empire of the Aztecs, as the ruling people of Mexico were called. The Aztecs had an impressive knowledge of arts and crafts and the Spaniards were amazed by the magnificence of their buildings. The greed of the Spaniards was aroused by the profusion of precious metals which they saw displayed on every side. But the Aztecs also practised human sacrifice, and the Spaniards considered that religion as well as the glory of their king demanded the conquest of the Aztec kingdom. After incredible adventures,[6] Cortes captured the city of Mexico (1521) and reduced the Aztec kingdom to a Spanish province.

Cortes was the first of the *Conquistadores* – the Spanish conquerors who built up Spain's overseas empire, men whose astonishing bravery and daring were matched only by their ruthlessness and cruelty. The cruellest and most successful of these Spanish adventurers was Pizarro, the conqueror of Peru (1532), who, with a handful of men, overthrew the Empire of the Incas. Thenceforth the silver mines of Peru unceasingly poured the precious metal into the coffers of Spain.

Pizarro

The astounding success of the Spaniards in the West was matched by the rapid progress of the Portuguese in the East. The founder of the Portuguese Empire was Albuquerque, who was sent out (1509) as Viceroy of the East. He and later the famous Jesuit missionary, St. Francis Xavier, became the heroes of a brilliant though short-lived empire. Albuquerque made Goa in India his headquarters, and shortly afterwards captured Malacca and the coveted Spice Islands. He made war on the Arabs, who had hitherto handled the trade of the Indian Ocean. Portuguese trading-posts were established at Mozambique and Madagascar, at Oman and Ormuz (in the Persian Gulf), in Ceylon, in the Spice Islands and Java. Trade was also begun

The Portuguese Eastern Empire

---

[6] Cortes made Montezuma, King of Mexico, his prisoner. The king was afterwards killed by his own people. See Rider Haggard's novel, *Montezuma's Daughter.*

with China (1517) and Japan (1542). The whole of the vast eastern trade went, year by year, round the Cape to Lisbon, which became the depot for the treasures of the East.

4. North America: Cabot and Cartier

The part played by England in the Age of Discovery seems small in comparison with the spectacular deeds of Spain and Portugal. While Henry VII was busy establishing order, the Portuguese were rounding the Cape and making a new way to the East, and Columbus was winning a new world for Spain. Henry VII, indeed, missed a great opportunity when Bartholomew Columbus, brother of the explorer, invited his assistance. Before Henry could make up his mind to accept the terms offered, Christopher Columbus had already sailed on his famous expedition in the Spanish service.

But there was in England another Italian navigator, Genoese-born, like Columbus himself. This was Giovanni Caboto, better known as John Cabot, a man who had had some experience of the East, and had travelled on the caravan routes through Central Asia to India. It was Cabot's belief that, although Columbus had failed to reach India by sailing southwest, the desired goal might be reached by sailing north-west instead; he thought that Cathay lay directly across the Atlantic.

John Cabot petitioned Henry VII for permission to sail an English ship across the Atlantic to put this theory to the test. He set sail (1497) from Bristol in a small ship with a crew of seventeen. He crossed the Atlantic in safety, and landed on an unknown shore, which was probably *New-found-land*. He was struck by the immense quantity of fish which he saw in this region, but otherwise he found nothing of value. He returned to England the same summer. There was great excitement in Bristol and London when it was known that Cabot had actually found land. No one doubted that he had reached

John Cabot

His first voyage to N. America 1497

Cathay: that he had, in fact, succeeded where Columbus had failed. 'Master John Caboto expects to go on', says a contemporary writer, until he shall be over against an island, called by him Cipango (Japan), where he thinks all the spices in the world and also all the precious stones originate.'

These were high hopes; and Cabot set out on his second voyage (1498) with five ships laden with bales of English cloth to exchange for the silks of Cathay. But Cabot, of course, saw neither Chinese junks nor Indian palaces; the inhospitable coast of North America, with its wooded shores stretching for mile after mile without sign of human habitation, must have been a bitter disappointment. The explorer returned, and confessed failure. The merchants who had invested in the enterprise suffered loss, and the enthusiasm for the new 'Route to India' rapidly cooled off. John Cabot died shortly afterwards. *Second voyage 1498*

Nevertheless, some attempts were made during the next few years to find a North-West Passage to Cathay, notably by Sebastian Cabot, son of John, who in 1509 explored the coast of Labrador. The chief result of the discovery of Newfoundland and Labrador was the opening of the cod fishery there, which both French and English fishermen sought to exploit. Their conflicts with each other in those fishing grounds were precursors of the long struggle that was to come between France and England in the New World. *Sebastian Cabot 1509*

Nearly twenty years after Cabot's voyage, Robert Thorne[7] son of a Bristol merchant, wrote a book called *A Declaration of the Indies*, which he sent to Henry VIII (1527). In this book Thorne urged the probable advantages – as he thought – of a North-West Passage to Asia, which he said would be a shorter route than that by the Cape or the Straits of Magellan. He also argued that, since the tropical regions had not proved too hot for Europeans, the Arctic would not prove too cold. One result of Thorne's *Declaration* was the sending *Robert Thorne*

---

[7] Thorne was the first Englishman to write a book on exploration.

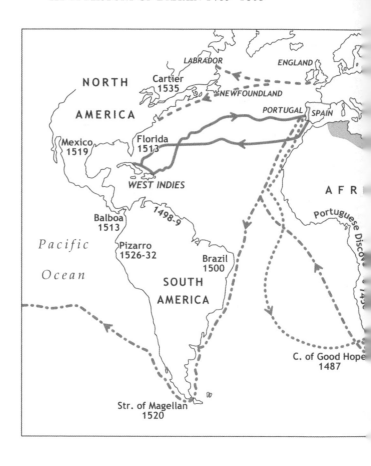

John Rut   of an expedition to the north-west in the same year, under John Rut,
1527   a master mariner of the Navy. Rut was turned back by the ice-fields
in the north, but he then sailed south down the shores of America till
he came to the West Indies. At Santo Domingo the Spaniards fired
on his ship – a foretaste of the reception which English sailors
experienced in Spanish waters in the days of Elizabeth.

But if the earliest efforts in the New World were disappointing, the
voyages of men like the Cabots foreshadowed subsequent events

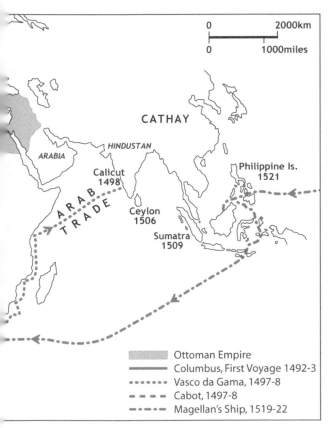

Ottoman Empire
Columbus, First Voyage 1492-3
Vasco da Gama, 1497-8
Cabot, 1497-8
Magellan's Ship, 1519-22

Voyages of Discovery,
1485-1535

which led to North America becoming an English-speaking continent. Nevertheless, the French were the first to colonize this part of the world. Jacques Cartier, the discoverer of Canada, was a French **Jacques Cartier** sailor, born at St. Malo, in Brittany. He made four voyages to the north-west, in the first of which he discovered (1534) the Gulf of St. Lawrence. On his second voyage he sailed right up the great river, **Canada 1534** which he named the St. Lawrence (1536). He came into contact with the native 'Red Indians', from one of whom he heard the name

Kanata or Canada – really the Indian name for a village. Cartier made two more voyages in the same locality. But it was not till the beginning of the next century in 1608 that Champlain founded the first French colony, Quebec, on the banks of the St. Lawrence.

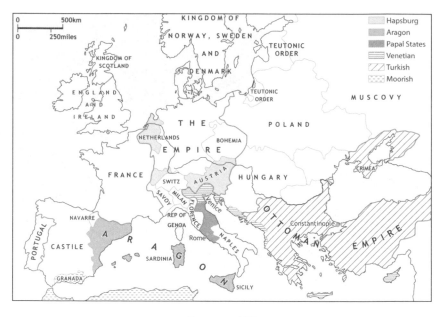

EUROPE IN 1490

II

THE RISE OF POWERFUL NATIONAL MONARCHIES

1. The Rise of National States

IN the Age of the Renaissance the Catholic ideal of the unity of all Christians finally broke down. In the middle Ages the Church and the Papacy had always stood for the unity of all Catholic Christians. Latin was an international language; and though the various peoples had their own languages, the continual use of Latin in both Church and State affairs helped educated men to regard themselves as members of one society, the society of Christendom. Above all, these peoples – English, French, Spanish, Italian, German – were all members of one Church. All belonged in some measure to Christendom, of which the spiritual head was the Pope. Gradually, in the 14th and 15th centuries, the idea that men's foremost loyalty was to the state took root, and this in time changed the unity of 'Christendom' into the disunion of 'Europe'. Modern Europe was to be divided into independent states; which soon no longer even shared the common bond of one Church. Only since the later 20th century have the jealous rivalries of warring European states come to be checked by the emergence of a new ideal of European unity, embodied in the European Union.

Idea of the Nation

The states which took the lead in Europe in the sixteenth, seventeenth, and eighteenth centuries were those that first achieved national unity, and the chief of these were France, Spain, and England. Italy, which had given so much to the world in art and letters, did not share in this political change. Italy was not a national state; but was divided into small states and was therefore often the

France, Spain, England

29

prey of powerful neighbours. Despite its ruler's possessing the title of Holy Roman Emperor, Germany contained three or four hundred separate states. Only in the 19th century did Germany and Italy become unified states.

Monarchy

The means by which national unity was brought about in France, Spain, and England was the monarchy. It was their kings who saved and made these countries – saved them from wars among the great nobles and made them into nations. It was monarchs like Henry VII and Henry VIII of England, Louis XI and Francis I of France, and Ferdinand and Isabella of Spain who united their countries under a strong rule, and led them to a great destiny. The Holy Roman Emperor Maximilian I (1493-1519) contrasted these monarchs with himself as follows: 'The Emperor is indeed a king of kings, for no one feels bound to obey him; and the King of Spain is a king of men, for, though resisted, he is still obeyed; but the King of France is a king of beasts, for him none dare gainsay.'

Machiavelli

The Age of the Renaissance certainly was not an age of political liberty. On the contrary, in many countries this was an age of rulers who took little account of their subjects' wishes. The generation which produced Michelangelo and Raphael also produced Machiavelli, the 'demon of politics'. This man saw the results of the French invasion of his country. All his life he dreamed of the union of Italy, and he wrote a book – *The Prince* – bearing on this problem. His book is a pitiless analysis of the methods by which an ambitious man, like Cesare Borgia in central Italy, could rise to power. According to Machiavelli, a successful politician achieves and keeps power by manipulating the people. In pursuit of success, a ruler has to be prepared to ignore the rules of morality and, when necessary, practise lying, fraud, cruelty, and murder. The interests of the state take precedence over all other considerations.

Not all Renaissance thinkers agreed with Machiavelli. Erasmus in his *Christian Prince* urged that there should be no distinction between political and Christian morality. Sir Thomas More in his work *Utopia* made his Utopians elect both their king and his council, though he confessed that 'there are many things in the commonwealth of Utopia that I rather wish than hope to see adopted in our own'.

2. Henry VII and the Tudor Monarchy

(i) *The Establishment of Order.*

When Henry VII came to the throne, the English had long been one people; what they needed was a strong government. This they could obtain only when the king kept in check the most powerful of his subjects, the great landowning nobles. The 'lack of governance' during the Wars of the Roses was followed by the effective rule of the Tudors. The Tudors were popular rulers in that their power was based on the co-operation of their people. Their work was sternly to establish order once and for all; and in asserting the royal will over both State and Church, they were wise enough to use Parliament to keep them in touch with the people.

Lack of governance

England, small and 'bound in with the triumphant sea', is a country which it is comparatively easy to unite under one rule; and it has been spared the worst evils of disunion which have, at different times, afflicted almost all continental countries. But the appearance of unity which England presented under medieval kings, like Edward I or Edward III, was always in danger of collapsing; for the medieval monarchy worked well only when the king was strong enough to control the barons. Henry V, who led a national English army to victory at Agincourt (1415), was the last king before the Tudors to keep his barons in order. After his death, the long dismal reign of his son, Henry VI (1422-61), saw England plunged into the struggle of rival factions which ended in civil war.

The country was tired of this chaotic state of affairs. For more than thirty years (1455-85) – if we except the latter half of the reign of Edward IV – there had been no stable government. The blessings

PORTRAIT, C. 1520, OF HENRY VII (1457-1509, REIGN: 1485-1509)

of peace and order were consequently lacking. These facts must be borne in mind in order to realize what it was that the Tudors achieved. They gave England internal order and peace, and saved it from civil war in their time.

The significance of the battle of Bosworth (1485), then, is that it ended the 'lack of governance' by putting a strong king on the throne. Henry Tudor, Earl of Richmond, landed in Wales on a doubtful enterprise, crossed England, and fought the king, Richard III, whose usurpation had divided the supporters of the Yorkist dynasty. Richard was killed at Bosworth; and the Tudor was hailed king as Henry VII.

Henry VII
1485-1509

The Tudors were a family which had only recently risen to prominence. The founder of the family fortunes was Owen Twydder or Tudor, a Welsh knight, who married Catherine of France, widow of Henry V. Owen's two sons, Edmund and Jasper, were made Earls of Richmond and Pembroke, respectively, by their half-brother, Henry VI. Edmund Tudor married Lady Margaret Beaufort, daughter of the Duke of Somerset; their only son was Henry Tudor. He was in exile while the Yorkist dynasty held the throne, but in 1485 he successfully invaded with French support.

Henry VII's claim to the throne, though not very strong, was fourfold: conquest, Parliament's declaration, the Pope's confirmation, and descent from John of Gaunt, third son of Edward III and ancestor of the House of Lancaster.[8] By descent, young Edward Plantagenet, Earl of Warwick (the son of Clarence, brother of Edward IV) was the rightful King of England. He was the only surviving male Plantagenet with an unbroken legitimate descent from Edward III. But the difference between Edward Plantagenet and Henry Tudor was this: Henry was sitting at Westminster wearing the Crown of England (which he had picked up from a hawthorn bush on Bosworth Field); Edward was a close prisoner in the Tower of London.

---

[8] See Table, p. 35.

The battle of Bosworth was won in August 1485; Henry VII was crowned in November. In the following January he married Elizabeth of York, eldest daughter of Edward IV, and thus brought about the union of the Red Rose of Lancaster and the White Rose of York. By this he hoped that Yorkist feeling would be pacified, but he was mistaken. The Yorkist cause found a redoubtable champion in Margaret, Duchess of Burgundy, sister of Edward IV. At the Burgundian court all Yorkist exiles found a welcome. The first attempt to overthrow Henry VII was made in 1487 by setting up a pretender, one Lambert Simnel, a baker's son, claiming to be the Earl of Warwick, who actually was in the Tower. Besides Flanders (ruled by the Duke of Burgundy), Ireland gave a welcome to pretenders; and Simnel was crowned king of England at Dublin. When he landed in England he was joined by John de la Pole, Earl of Lincoln (a nephew of Edward IV), and by other Yorkists. At the battle (1487) of Stoke (near Newark), Lincoln was slain. This was the last battle of the Wars of the Roses: it ended the period of civil war which had started at the battle of St Alban's in 1455. Simnel was taken prisoner, and to show his contempt for him Henry employed him in the royal kitchens.

The Yorkists then found another pretender, named Perkin Warbeck, who claimed to be Richard, Duke of York, brother of Edward V, alleging that he had escaped when his brother was murdered. Warbeck gave Henry some anxiety for nearly a dozen years. He visited in turn most of Henry's enemies – first Flanders, then Ireland, and afterwards Scotland. James IV, who was not yet on good terms with Henry, gave him a Scottish wife. At last he landed in England (1497), but was promptly seized and brought before the king. After two years' imprisonment, he was executed on a further charge of conspiracy. With him perished the young and innocent Earl of Warwick, who was condemned on a trumped-up charge, and sent to a cruel and quite unmerited death (1499). Henry, who was then negotiating a marriage between his elder son Arthur and the daughter of the King of Spain, wanted Warwick out of the way because the

Marriage of Henry VII 1485

Revolts against his rule 1487-99

Warbeck and Warwick

THE HOUSES OF LANCASTER, YORK AND TUDOR

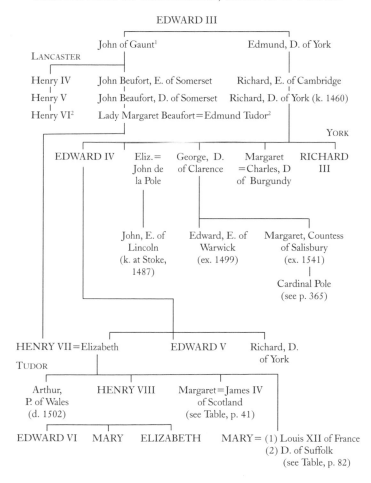

---

[1] For Table showing, more fully, the family of John of Gaunt, see previous column.
[2] Sons of Catherine of France. See p. 33.

Spaniards were nervous of Yorkist claimants to the Tudor throne. The blameless Warwick's only crime was that he was the last direct male representative of the Plantagenet kings of England.

The policy of Henry VII throughout his reign was to prevent any challenge to his rule from the nobility. He was well aware that over-mighty subjects had brought the Lancastrian monarchy to ruin. Fortunately for the Tudor monarchy, the Wars of the Roses had considerably thinned the ranks of claimants to the throne. Of other nobles, Henry VII fully trusted very few, perhaps only his uncle Jasper Tudor and the Earl of Oxford, both of whom had been in exile with him before 1485. Yet he could not do without the nobles' help in raising armies and ruling the localities where they had influence. Henry therefore sought to gain a hold over the great lords which would make opposition a very dangerous undertaking for them. Hence the Howard family, deprived of lands and titles for opposing Henry at Bosworth, was given a strong incentive to serve faithfully by gradual and partial restoration as it rendered service to the King. Other nobles suspected by the King were forced to acknowledge liability to huge fines, which would have to be paid as soon as they stepped out of line. To his Council of advisors Henry, like his predecessors, promoted men of ability, whatever their social origin: some of them, like the Howard Earl of Surrey, were nobles, others were churchmen like Archbishop Morton, and yet others were lawyers recruited from the lesser landowners.

Henry and the nobility

Henry VII passed laws to punish offences to which great men were particularly prone: keeping liveried retainers who could become the nucleus of a private army and 'maintaining' their followers' causes in the courts by frightening juries, i.e. the two offences known as 'Livery' and 'Maintenance'. Of course, enforcing laws was more difficult than passing them. Only Henry's Council, composed of his chief advisors, was adequate to the task. It was to be Henry VIII's chief minister Cardinal Wolsey who followed up the work of the first Tudor by using the Council to teach the great men of the kingdom that everyone must obey the law of the land. In his time when the Council met as a court, it assembled in a room with stars painted on the ceiling. Consequently, it became known as the Court of Star Chamber. Henry VII also revived two other special courts – the Council of the North and the Council of Wales – to deal with disturbances in the most distant portions of his kingdom.

Star Chamber

Henry VII was thrifty by nature, and he accumulated a large treasure, much of it in the form of jewels and plate. Towards the end of his reign, he employed two lawyers, named Empson and Dudley. These 'ravening wolves' used every means which ingenuity could devise to extort money from the king's subjects and to enrich their master. The city of London had to pay heavily to have its liberties confirmed (1505). Sir William Capell, a former Lord Mayor of London, was 'put on examination by the suit of the king for things done by him in the time of his mayoralty', fined £2,000, and sent to the Tower. The smallest infraction of the law was punished by heavy fines, and no man could feel safe from the king's agents. Henry VII encouraged these odious methods, for he specially desired to secure his throne against poverty – hence his so-called avarice. But his was not a reign of blood. Henry preferred money.

Empson and Dudley

(ii) *Commercial and Foreign Policy.*

The Tudors did much to mould the destiny of England by their commercial policy. The first of the Tudors was himself an astute man of business. 'He could not endure to see trade sick,' wrote Francis Bacon, his biographer. He worked hard to promote the interests of his merchants and traders and so to increase the wealth and power of the country and hence his own revenues, a large proportion of which came from customs duties. Before his time, it was mainly foreign ships and foreign merchants that carried away English wool and half-made cloth and brought back European and eastern goods. Henry VII's policy sought to develop the two main industries of cloth-working and shipping, which remained the basis of England's wealth till the nineteenth century.

Navigation
Act 1485

In order to build up a Merchant Navy, he passed a new Navigation Act (1485), which ordained that the Bordeaux wines brought to this country were to be carried only in English ships, manned by English, Irish, or Welsh sailors. He also aimed a blow at the powerful Hanseatic League of German towns that controlled the trade of the North Sea and the Baltic by making commercial treaties with the port of Riga and with Denmark to give English ships access to the Baltic trade. The later Tudors gradually weakened the hold of the Hanseatic League on England, and then at last England became commercially an independent country.

Further, Henry VII made commercial treaties with the Italian States, to encourage English ships to trade in the Mediterranean. Hitherto, Venetian galleys and Genoese carracks had been almost the only carriers of goods to England from the Mediterranean. Now, for the first time, English traders began to make regular voyages to the distant eastern Mediterranean – then an enterprise of great danger and difficulty because of the north African pirates-and to trade in the spices of the East. This Levant voyage was the first really long trade-route of the English.

The Navy

Thus Henry VII won for Englishmen the right to carry their wares in English ships wherever they wished. We have seen, too how he encouraged the Cabots in their ocean voyages. Nor did the king's activity stop here. He caused to be built, at his own expense, several fine ships for use in war or trade, which exceeded in size any hitherto seen in English harbours. Henry VIII continued his father's work and together they laid the basis of England's sea-power.

Besides developing shipping, Henry VII did much to encourage the trade in English woollen cloth, for which there was a great demand abroad. The trading company known as the Merchant Adventurers included the chief cloth-exporters; and their trade in cloth had increased ten times in volume since Edward III's time.

This meant an increasing demand for wool, which led to further enclosures of ploughland into sheep-runs. But sheep-grazing needs fewer labourers than arable farming, and so these enclosures were blamed for causing serious unemployment among ploughmen. Tudor statesmen – especially Sir Thomas More, and Somerset – were much concerned about this problem of enclosures, and it played a part in almost every insurrection of Tudor times.

Henry found the prosperity of the Merchant Adventurers endangered by the enmity of the Duchess Margaret, the Yorkist princess and harbourer of Yorkist pretenders. He therefore moved their staple, or chief market, from Antwerp to Calais, and this soon brought the Flemish to reason. Then Henry made the commercial treaty known as 'Magnus Intercursus' (1496), or The Great Intercourse, by which he obtained a free market 'without pass or licence' for English cloth in Flanders.

Flanders Trade

By making England more self-supporting in its cloth and shipping industries Henry VII hoped to make his country more independent and more powerful. His success was only partial. England remained overwhelmingly dependent on one industry, cloth-making, and one export market, Antwerp in the Netherlands. Most Englishmen still earned their living from agriculture, but English agricultural production remained only a fraction of the output of its huge neighbour France.

Mercantile system

In his dealings with foreign countries, and with the one English dependency, Ireland, Henry showed his usual foresight. To Ireland he sent Sir Edward Poynings, a member of the King's Council, who induced the Irish Parliament, which met at Drogheda in 1494, to pass a series of Acts (known as Poynings' Laws). They subordinated the Irish Parliament to royal control. Henry's aim was to prevent Irish support for pretenders to his crown. Once he had achieved his aim by 1496, Henry allowed the great Irish noble, the Earl of Kildare, to govern Ireland in his name. With Scotland, Henry negotiated a royal marriage, designed to promote peace between the

Ireland

two countries and destined in due course to unite the two Crowns.

Henry's eldest daughter, Margaret, was wedded to the King of Scots, James IV in 1502; and from that marriage came the Stuart dynasty which ruled England after 1603.

Henry VII was, as has been seen, a man of peace. His one and only foreign war was of short duration, and not notable for military glory. Charles VIII of France was engaged in subduing the hitherto independent duchy of Brittany – an object which Henry wished to prevent. He therefore induced Parliament to grant him a large sum of money to invade France; he landed and besieged Boulogne; then he accepted an even larger sum from Charles VIII to make peace and return home (Treaty of Etaples, 1492). Henry took no further part in continental wars, but left the Frenchmen and Spaniards to cut each other's throats in Italy.

Henry VII had to reckon with the great powers that arose in Europe in his time – France, Spain, and the Habsburg Empire. These three powers were bent on the conquest of Italy, whose petty states made it a prey to the invader – and invaded it was by Charles VIII of France in 1494. All three powers sought the friendship of Henry VII. It was in this way that England became involved in a system of dynastic marriages, i.e. marriages between royal houses by which monarchs built up great inheritances and treated countries as though they were family estates.

First had come the Spanish marriage (1469) of Ferdinand and Isabella by which their two kingdoms of Aragon and Castile were united; of this marriage there were two daughters, Joanna and Catherine. Secondly, there was the marriage (1477) of Maximilian I, by which the Austrian Habsburgs obtained the Burgundian lands including the Netherlands; and of this marriage there was a son, Philip the Fair. Thirdly, in Henry VII's time, there was the Austrian-Spanish marriage (1496), by which the Austrian Philip the Fair married the Spanish Joanna; and they had a son, Charles. This Charles was in 1519 elected Emperor as Charles V, and he inherited

THE DYNASTIC MARRIAGES

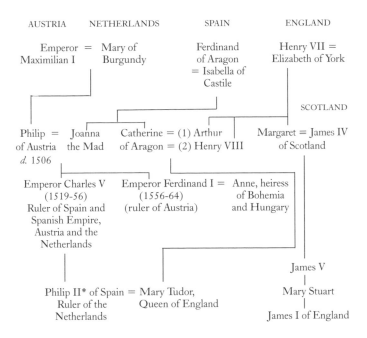

* Note: Philip II inherited all the Habsburg lands except those in Austria and Germany, which went to his uncle Ferdinand, who also became Emperor.

all the vast lands of his four grandparents. Thus royal marriages were of great importance, for upon them hung the history of Europe in the Tudor Age. (See Table above.)

Marriage of Prince Arthur 1501

What prize was Henry VII to have as the price of his friendship? An Anglo-Spanish marriage was arranged; Henry's elder son Arthur was betrothed to Catherine of Aragon. This marriage did not actually take place for some years, partly because the kings haggled for a long time over the dowry. 'No sharp-witted, close-fisted huckster chaffering his wares at a country fair could have shown a keener desire to save a halfpenny than the King of England, and no peasants who ever drove their cart to market were more sharp-witted and closefisted than the King and Queen of Spain.'[9] The marriage at last took place (1501); five months afterwards Prince Arthur died. Henry VII, anxious not to lose Catherine's dowry, then suggested that the princess should be betrothed to his younger son Henry, now Prince of Wales. A papal dispensation was obtained (1503), for without it a man could not marry his brother's widow. This marriage, so ominous for the course of English history, did not, however, take place in Henry VII's lifetime. The king died in 1509, and was buried in the beautiful Italian tomb in his Chapel at Westminster Abbey.

3. Henry VIII, Wolsey, and Europe

Henry VIII
1509-47

The accession of Henry VIII (1509) was hailed with joy in England. The young king was eighteen years old, well educated, of fine physique, an adept at sports, and apparently good-natured. Few if any men saw in this handsome, sport-loving boy the signs of his future development. The keen intellect and the ruthless, unbending will were alike hidden from those who observed the king in his youth. And, indeed, the legend of 'Bluff King Hal' has been preserved to this day. But whoever has stood before Holbein's portrait of Henry, painted in about 1536, and noted the cold eyes staring from the heavy face, and seen that small, cruel mouth, has seen Henry VIII as he was in later life.

Henry's first action on ascending the throne was a popular one. His father's hated ministers, Empson and Dudley, were arrested on

---

[9] *Pol. Hist. Eng.* v (H. A. L. Fisher).

the day of his accession; they were tried for treason and executed. In June the King married Catherine of Aragon. Two years later the Queen gave birth to a son, who did not live a month. This was to prove the first of a series of disappointments for the King and Queen.

The first twenty years (1509-29) of Henry's reign, when Wolsey was his chief minister, were concerned largely with foreign affairs. Since 1494 Italy had been the cockpit of Europe, and there the armies of France and Spain fought for the mastery of the peninsula. Though Wolsey attempted much, England could do little to affect the result.

Two years after Henry VIII's accession, in 1511, the warlike Pope, Julius II, formed the Holy League with Spain to check the French advance in Italy. Henry VIII also joined it, in the hope of recovering the lost English province of Gascony. In this manner the king turned his mind to the old dream of a continental empire, though Dean Colet and others among his subjects dared to protest against this folly. Henry's first expedition against France was a complete failure. The second was commanded by the king in person. He landed at Calais, took a few towns, and met a French army at a skirmish called the Battle of the Spurs (1513), from the fact that his opponents fled at the first encounter. It was not much of a victory, perhaps, but it was the first success for English arms in Europe for ninety years.

Henry and France

Meanwhile James IV of Scotland took advantage of Henry's absence to invade England. He preferred to follow the old Scottish policy of the French alliance, rather than to pursue the new peace policy expected from his marriage with Margaret Tudor. James paid for this venture with his life. At the battle of Flodden (1513) near the Tweed, the Earl of Surrey won a crushing victory over the Scots, James and all his chief lords being left dead on the field. For this, Surrey was made Duke of Norfolk.

Battle of Flodden 1513

Henry had entrusted the preparations for his French war to Thomas Wolsey. This rising man was the son of a grazier. He was educated at the Grammar School of his native Ipswich, and at Magdalen

Wolsey

DETAIL FROM (C. 1554) PORTRAIT OF HENRY VIII AND FAMILY.
From left to right: Prince Edward, Henry VIII and Jane Seymour.

College, Oxford, where he took his degree at the age of fifteen. He afterwards entered the Church, and, gaining the favour of the influential Bishop Fox, was made Dean of Lincoln and chaplain to the king. He won Henry VIII's favour by his obvious abilities, and was rewarded in 1514 with the bishopric of Lincoln and the archbishopric of York. The next year (1515) Wolsey was appointed Chancellor, and was made a cardinal by the new Pope, Leo X. His influence on his royal master soon became enormous; and many contemporaries commented on his pride and arrogance. The Venetian ambassador thus described him: 'He is very handsome, learned, extremely eloquent and of vast ability. He alone transacts the same business as that which occupies all the officers and councils of Venice. He is in very great repute, seven times more so than if he were Pope. He is the person who rules both the king and the entire kingdom.' Wolsey himself was always aware that his power depended entirely on pleasing the King.

In accordance with Henry's wishes, Wolsey was determined to cut a figure in Europe and to assert the voice of England in European affairs. Since Spain had not given Henry adequate support in his war with France, he and Wolsey exchanged their alliance with Spain for one with France. It was sealed by the marriage of Louis XII, aged 52, with Henry's sister, Mary, aged 18. Louis died shortly afterwards, however, and the alliance could not survive the accession of a young and glamorous King of France, Francis I, who aroused Henry's jealousy by winning a great victory in North Italy at Marignano in 1515. Wolsey needed to win glory for his master and he succeeded by inducing all the powers of Europe to sign a treaty of peace at London in 1518. The Pope rewarded him with a grant of extra powers over the Church in England.

Meanwhile, Henry's father-in-law, Ferdinand of Aragon died in 1516, and then in 1519 the Emperor Maximilian also died. When these figures had passed from the scene, Francis I of France and the Emperor Charles V, young men like the English king, were Henry's and Wolsey's antagonists in the European battle of wits. The rise of

Wolsey's foreign policy

France and the Empire

Charles V
1519-56

the House of Habsburg was of outstanding importance in European history. The Emperor Charles V had inherited large though scattered masses of territory (see map), which gave him control of a considerable part of Europe. From his *maternal* grandparents (Ferdinand and Isabella) he inherited Spain, the New World, and the Spanish possessions in Italy; from his *paternal* grandparents (Maximilian of Austria and Mary of Burgundy) he inherited the Habsburg lands in Austria, Burgundy, and the Netherlands. (See Table, p. 41.) His possessions lay on two sides of France, which allied itself against him with German princes and even the Turks.

Given the rivalry of Francis I and Charles V, peace could not long survive. Both rulers bid for English support in the coming war between them. Wolsey arranged an amicable meeting between Henry and Francis I. It took place in 1520 near Guisnes, and was known, from the magnificence of the display, as the Field of Cloth of Gold. But Henry also had two interviews with his nephew Charles V, one before and one after his meeting with Francis, and he concluded a

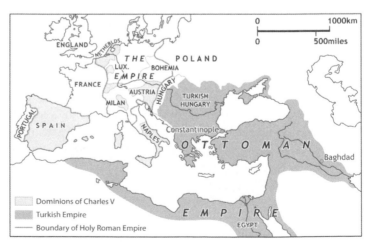

EUROPE AND ASIA MINOR IN THE TIME OF CHARLES V

secret treaty with him against France. Francis was not surprised when England declared war against him (1522); he was already at war with the Emperor.

Henry sent an army to France, which achieved nothing. The war was expensive and unpopular in England. Wolsey received a rebuff at the hands of Parliament in 1523, when the members refused to discuss war-taxation until he left the House, and then voted much less than the amount he had demanded. Two years later in 1525, Francis I was defeated by Charles V at Pavia, in Italy, and taken prisoner. Henry and Wolsey then judged that the time was opportune for another invasion of France. They did not risk summoning another Parliament, but tried to raise an 'Amicable Loan', which was really a tax on property. Henry ensured that Wolsey took the blame for this unpopular and unsuccessful measure: 'All people cursed the Cardinal' for subverting 'the laws and liberties of England'. As the loan nearly led to a rebellion, it was decided to reverse the policy and make peace again with France (1525). Francis agreed to buy Henry's friendship for two million crowns.

Battle of
Pavia 1525

When Francis I was released from captivity he renewed his treaty with England, and Wolsey abandoned the imperial alliance. There were several reasons for this change of policy. Wolsey was disappointed at not being made Pope, for Charles had lent his support to a Medici cardinal, now Clement VII. Above all, Charles V had done nothing for his English ally in the recent war with France. Charles's successes, however, were not yet over. When Clement VII formed a new league against him, his German troops sacked the Holy City (1527), which now suffered more from a Christian army than it had ever done from pagan barbarians.

Sack of
Rome 1527

The Pope became the Emperor's prisoner. It was at this disastrous moment that Henry began negotiations with the Pope to divorce Catherine, the Emperor's aunt. The conduct of this business was given to Wolsey. His failure to carry it through brought about his downfall, and led on to Henry VIII's break with the Papacy and the subsequent reformation of the English Church. Altogether, the results of Wolsey's diplomacy were disappointing. All the Cardinal's astuteness could not make up for England's inability to project its power into Italy, nor for the smallness of Henry's revenues compared with the resources available to Francis I and Charles V.

4. Henry VIII and the Navy

The reign of Henry VIII may be divided into two periods. The first period from 1509 to 1529 was marked by the ascendancy of Wolsey, the second by Henry's breach with the Papacy.

There was one factor which was common to both periods – the King's unremitting care for the Royal Navy. While Balboa was viewing the Pacific, while Magellan's men were sailing round the world, while Cortes was conquering Mexico, and Pizarro exploiting the silver mines of Peru, Henry VIII was laying the foundations of his country's greatness on the sea.

The Merchant Navy

English ships, in early medieval times, were not divided into fighting ships and merchantmen. All were merchantmen, and all were armed – against pirates in time of peace, and, more heavily, against the enemy in time of war. When an English king requisitioned ships to cross the Channel in a French war his officers built wooden 'castles' at either end of the ship: from these castles both arrows and the first small guns were fired. Early in the fifteenth century, some ships were being built for war only. Then, by the reign of Henry VIII, there was a great improvement in artillery, and Henry ordered large cannon from the Netherlands. It soon became obvious that the new large guns were too heavy for the 'castles'. James Baker, 'skilful in ships', is said to have been the first naval architect to adapt English ships to carry heavy guns; and at the beginning of Henry VIII's reign the idea was suggested of piercing holes (called port-holes from French porte) in the vessel's side, through which the guns might be fired. Thus was invented the famous 'broadside'.

Henry was an enthusiastic ship-builder. He inherited from his father seven ships, two large and five small. By the end of his reign he had increased this number to fifty-three. The largest ship he built, the *Henry Grace à Dieu*, or the *Great Harry*, was of 1,500 tons. All these ships were heavily armed with the new guns, the like of which were destined to defeat the Spanish Armada. Just as important among the naval innovations of the reign was the creation of the Navy Board, whose function was to maintain, supply and man the new fleet.

The Royal Navy

The French wars of Henry's reign produced no very striking naval battle. In the first war Sir Edward Howard won the command of the Channel in a battle off Brest (1512). In the second war the French did not put to sea. Twenty years later, right at the end of the reign, there was a third war. The Scots, as usual, were allied with the French. James V sent an army across the border, which was defeated by Sir Thomas Wharton at the battle of Solway Moss (1542). The French galleys attacked Portsmouth, where they tried to land, but the next day they rowed away without a battle; the existence of Henry's new fleet saved England from an invasion (1545) more carefully planned than any since the Norman Conquest.

And so the power of the new sea weapon was not put to a decisive test till Elizabeth's day. The English broadsides were to prove vastly superior to the Mediterranean method of warfare – which dated back to the days of the Greeks and Persians. The chief naval powers of the Mediterranean, Spain and Venice, both used the long galley, rowed by slaves, depending first on its formidable beak for ramming other ships, and secondly on its capacity to carry soldiers to board the enemy. But Henry's ships carried weapons against which the methods of galley warfare were powerless – as was seen later when Drake, with the successors of Henry's ships, won his victory at Cadiz. Thus Henry VIII had effected a revolution in naval warfare. He was the true founder of the Royal Navy, as his father Henry VII was of the merchant navy.

The English broadsides

Lutheran
Angican
Calvinist
Roman Catholic

NORWAY

SWEDEN

SCOTLAND

IRELAND

DENMARK

ENGLAND

NETHERLANDS

POLAND

BOHEMIA

SWITZ.

AUSTRIA

Greek Orthodox
Church
(Turkish
Conquest)

ITALY

PORTUGAL

SPAIN

Rome

ISLAMIC

0   500km

0   250miles

THE REFORMATION

III

THE REFORMATION IN EUROPE

1. Erasmus and More

THE thirty years (1492-1521) between the crossing of the Atlantic by Columbus and the crossing of the Pacific by Magellan were also momentous years in the history of the Church. Three famous Popes lived in this period: Alexander VI, Julius II, and Leo X. Their reigns were remarkable in many ways. It was Alexander VI who divided the New World between Spain and Portugal, and who sent the reformer Savonarola to the flames. Julius II played an important part in European politics and he himself fought to establish the control of the Church over central Italy, putting on armour, and proudly riding his war-horse under fire. Leo X, the patron of Michelangelo and Raphael, inspired great achievements in the realm of art; but the 'indulgence' that he sanctioned to raise funds for re-building St. Peter's provoked Luther's revolt. Neither the patronage of art and letters nor the building of St. Peter's could blind men to the fact that these Popes did not model themselves on Jesus and his disciples. It was this contrast between the early Church and the Church of the 16th century that caused the voices of reformers to be raised in protest.

About the time that Colet at Oxford was exhorting men to imitate the life of Christ, another reformer, Friar Savonarola of Florence, was fervently denouncing the corruptions of the Church and winning a great following. After the expulsion of the Medici in 1494, this friar became for a time the real ruler of Florence. He even persuaded the people to make a bonfire of their pictures, jewels, and immoral books in a public square, and he thundered against the scandalous life of Pope Alexander. But the friar's popularity soon waned. Then Alexander suppressed the dangerous preacher, who in 1498 was

The Renaissance Popes

Savonarola

condemned as a heretic and burnt in the presence of the fickle multitude.

Erasmus   Amongst other reformers was Erasmus. Born in Rotterdam, he acquired an international reputation as a scholar. When he was in his thirties he came to England (1499) – in Henry VII's reign – and made the acquaintance of Colet, and of More, then a young man of twenty. The friendship of these three men endured for the rest of their lives, and it will remain forever memorable in the history of European thought. At the accession of Henry VIII, Erasmus for a time made England his home, and at Cambridge he lectured on Divinity and Greek. His friend Colet, as Dean of St. Paul's, did not fear to preach before Henry VIII against the king's own foreign policy, and as lecturer in Greek at Oxford and founder of St. Paul's School, he did much to forward the New Learning.

But it was not merely by attacking outworn methods of teaching that these great scholars played their part. As reformers they were the leaders of their time. Erasmus, in particular, was disgusted at the lack of spiritual leadership at Rome. 'I saw with my own eyes,' he wrote, 'Pope Julius II at Rome, marching at the head of a triumphal procession, as if he were Pompey or Caesar. St. Peter subdued the world by faith, not with arms or soldiers or military engines.' In his *Praise of Folly* (1510) Erasmus satirized kings and princes, Pope and clergy, especially the monks, of whose way of life he had conceived a strong dislike during his own time as a monk in his early years.

Erasmus'   In 1516 Erasmus published his scholarly edition of the New
New   Testament, recreating as far as possible the Greek original by
Testament   comparison of early manuscripts, and adding a Latin translation and
1516   annotations of his own. The object of this great work was to bring the actual words and teaching of the Scriptures before men. Erasmus hoped that men would read and understand the Bible, that 'the peasant should sing bits of it as he followed the plough, and that the weaver should hum them to the tune of his shuttle'. Both Erasmus and the reformers at Oxford sought to guide the Church back to the

ideals of its Founder as portrayed in the New Testament; they used the New Learning to promote a Christian Renaissance; but, unlike Luther, they had no desire to cut themselves adrift from the Church of Rome.

About the same time that Erasmus was translating the New Testament, another reformer, Sir Thomas More, was writing a book which he called *Utopia*. More was a Londoner, born in 1478 in Milk Street, Cheapside. As a boy he entered the service of Archbishop Morton, through whose influence he was sent to Canterbury Hall, Oxford, which was afterwards merged in Wolsey's college of Christ Church. It was at Oxford that the young student became influenced by the New Learning, and there that he afterwards met Colet and Erasmus. His father decided that he should enter his own profession, the law, and More left Oxford to become a student at the bar in London. His legal career was a brilliant success; and he was a notable Speaker of the House of Commons in 1523. But, in spite of the cares of official work, More found time to keep up his friendship with Colet and Erasmus, and it was largely owing to Colet's influence that he wrote his great book.

Utopia, (*Nowhere* in Greek), which was written in Latin, is one of the famous books of the world. It was an account of the ideas which inspired the three friends in their hopes for the future, and was at the same time a satire on the existing state of society. These Oxford reformers were all sincere Christians and good Catholics. They believed that the new ideas of the Renaissance and its Greek and Latin scholarship might be combined with the ideals of the Christian faith. They were shocked at the semi-paganism of Rome and Italy; they wished to see, not the Church overthrown from without, but the Church reformed from within.

In his book More goes farther than imagining a reformed Church: he pictures a reformed world. The description of his imaginary country he puts into the mouth of a sailor who was supposed to have returned from a long voyage to the New World. In place of the filthy

Sir Thomas More

Utopia

streets of European towns More imagined a land with well-built houses, properly ventilated and surrounded by well-kept gardens, with hospitals, waterworks, and halls for the public use. In contrast to Europeans, 'The Utopians hate war as plainly brutal, although practised more eagerly by man than by any other animal.' In Europe, wrote the author in an ironic passage, 'where the Christian faith and religion are practised, the sanctity of leagues is held sacred and inviolate', but the truth was, of course, that European treaties were often broken almost as soon as they were made.

Rich and poor
With the sufferings of the poor, as More saw them in Tudor England, he showed a keen sympathy. 'Our modern republics,' he wrote, 'are nothing but a conspiracy of the rich. The poor are left uneducated, too often brought up in haunts of crime and vice, then punished for becoming thieves and vagabonds.' He commented on the number of thieves hanged in England – 'for the most part twenty hanged together on one gallows, and I cannot but marvel that thieves nevertheless are in every place so rife and so rank.'

Enclosures
One of the most famous passages describes the evils which, according to More, resulted from the 'enclosure' of land in England – a process which Wolsey had tried to check. In the interests of the cloth industry, he claimed, large areas of land were being enclosed for sheep farms, with the result that whole villages were falling into decay.

'Your sheep that were wont to be so meek and tame, and so small eaters, now be become so great devourers and so wild, that they eat up and swallow down the very men themselves' (i.e. sheep farms put men out of work). 'For noblemen and gentlemen, yea, and certain abbots, holy men no doubt, leave no ground for tillage: they enclose all into pastures: they throw down houses: they pluck down towns, and leave nothing standing, but only the church to be made a sheep-house. In order that one covetous and insatiable cormorant and the very plague of his native country may enclose many thousand acres

SIR THOMAS MORE (1478-1535)
(1527 portrait by Hans Holbein.)

of ground within one pale or hedge, the ploughmen be thrust out of their own.'

Not long after the publication of *Utopia* More was promoted into the royal service – dragged, rather, says Erasmus, 'for no one ever struggled harder to gain admission there than More struggled to escape'. Henry VIII was charmed, as better men than he were, by the gentleness of More's character, and by the brilliance of his wit. He showed the able lawyer great favour. Although the king was not then the odious tyrant he afterwards became, More made no mistake about his true character. 'If my head should win him a castle in France', he remarked to his son-in-law, 'it should not fail to go.'

2. Luther and the German Reformation

It was not, however, by a Utopian reformation in laws and manners that the world was to be changed; nor by a peaceful reform of the Church which Erasmus and More so much desired. The evils of the time – the worldliness of popes, the selfishness of princes, the ignorance of the people – were plain enough for all to see. But these evils may be likened to fermenting agents: they led, not to a peaceful change, but to an explosion – a revolution. The man whose career most influenced the outbreak of this revolution was Martin Luther (1483-1546), the friar who shook the world.

Martin
Luther
1483-1546

Luther was born at Eisleben in Saxony. His father had prospered in the mining industry and managed to send his clever son to Erfurt University. A few years later Martin suddenly renounced the world and entered a friary at Erfurt,[10] where the religious life was strictly upheld. A visitor to the friary, struck by his learning and earnestness, procured his removal to the new Saxon University of Wittenberg, where for ten years he was lecturer in theology. It was during this period in 1511 that Luther was sent to Rome on a mission, and there he was horrified, like Erasmus, at the worldly lives of the Pope and

---

[10] Luther was not, strictly speaking, a monk (as he is often called), but one of the Augustinian Friars, who lived under a rule much like that of the monks.

MARTIN LUTHER (1483-1546)
(1532 portrait by Lucas Cranach)

Cardinals. 'The Italians,' he said, 'make sport of the true religion; and they rail at us Christians because we believe everything in the Scriptures.'

Then came the fateful year 1517; though no one, least of all Luther himself, realized that in that year he was to begin a world revolution. The Pope, Leo X, was in need of money for the re-building of St. Peter's – a laudable enough object. Collections were made for the purpose in Germany; and money was raised by the grant of indulgences. Indulgences granted the removal of the punishment due in this life and after death for sins committed to those who confessed their guilt and expressed true sorrow for what they had done. A Dominican friar named Tetzel was commissioned to sell indulgences near Wittenberg. When he entered a German town for this purpose, the priests and monks, the town council, the teachers and scholars, and a crowd of citizens escorted him with banners and lighted candles and hymns. With bells ringing and the organ playing, the procession entered the principal church, where a great cross was erected and the Pope's banner displayed. Then after a sermon the sales began.

Tetzel in Germany 1517

The issue of indulgences was a very old custom connected with the Catholic sacrament of penance, and Luther, like other churchmen, believed that at its basis there was a great truth. But, in the hands of Tetzel, the sale of indulgences became an open scandal, for he offered them to all who paid, without stressing sufficiently the need for penitence. He gave out that 'as soon as the coin rang in the chest, the soul for whom the money was paid would go straightway to heaven'. Many thoughtful people besides Luther were revolted by this abuse of the practice. Erasmus, for instance, had recently written: 'The Court of Rome clearly has lost all sense of shame; for what could be more shameless than these continued indulgences?' It was left for Martin Luther to deliver a blow at this abuse which in due course shook the whole papal system. He was disgusted at Tetzel's behaviour. He therefore wrote out ninety-five theses (i.e. topics for discussion) attacking the abuses. He nailed his theses to the church door at Wittenberg. The effect was tremendous: the growing protest against the worldliness of the Church and the desire for its reform

Indulgences

Luther's theses 1517

now centred upon Luther. Yet at the time Pope Leo X thought it was all a joke – 'friars wrangling as usual', as he remarked; 'as usual', for there had, of course, been many disputes over points of theology before Luther.

It is doubtful whether Luther knew where he was going when he launched his attack, and none goes so far as he who knows not whither he is going. But by 1520 he had gone very far indeed. Efforts to silence him made him all the more stubborn and he began to attack the supremacy of the Pope, who tried to use his authority against him. Luther was using violent words: 'If,' he said, 'we strike thieves with the gallows and the sword, why do we not much more attack in arms these masters of perdition, these Cardinals, these Popes and all this sink which has corrupted the Church of God?' His words were spread throughout Germany by the agency of the printing press, without which it is doubtful whether his attack on the Papacy would have met with the success that it did.

History presents no greater contrast in character than that between the Medici Pope, Leo X, and his great German antagonist. Luther was passionate and highly strung, but he was an honest man, who upheld what he saw as the truth even when it proved to be a path to revolution. The world of Leo X was far removed from him. To Luther the builder of St. Peter's and the patron of Michelangelo was a worldly prince who robbed honest Germans in order to live in luxury and who had perverted the Gospel of Christ. Leo understood Luther as little as Luther understood him. The cultured, kindly, ease-loving Pope had little idea of the forces behind the wrangling friar. *Leo X and Luther*

In 1520 the Pope issued a Bull of Excommunication against Luther. Public opinion in Germany enabled Luther to defy the Pope: he burnt the Papal Bull in the market-place at Wittenberg. At this act of open defiance the defenders of the old order stood aghast. The following year Luther was cited to appear before the Diet (Parliament) of the Holy Roman Empire at Worms (on the Rhine). *The Papal Bull 1520*

The young Emperor, Charles V, gave him a safe-conduct, and Luther obeyed the summons. His friends warned him of the fate of John Hus at the Council of Constance, who (a hundred years before) had been burnt as a heretic in spite of the Emperor Sigismund's safe-conduct. 'I will go', replied Luther, 'though every tile in the city is a devil.'

Diet of Worms

At the Diet of Worms (1521) Luther was asked to recant the opinions which he had uttered and published. He replied that he dared not act against the Bible and his conscience which told him he was right. From this position he would not move: 'Here I stand. I can do no other. God help me. Amen.' Luther, in thus setting up 'the Bible and the Bible only' against the authority of the Catholic Church, defined that attitude to religion which was afterwards called Protestant, though the word itself was not coined until 1529.

In that same fateful year of 1521 Henry VIII wrote his *Assertio Septem Sacramentorum* (*Defence of the Seven Sacraments*), refuting Luther's arguments. He sent the book to Leo X who awarded him the title of *Fidei Defensor, 'Defender of the Faith'*. This title the kings of England still retain, as we are reminded by the inscription on our coins – F.D. Shortly afterwards Leo died, unaware that the old united Christendom was about to crash in ruins.

Luther's Bible

On leaving Worms, Luther was protected by his supporter the Elector of Saxony, who guarded him in his castle of Wartburg. Here Luther occupied his days in translating the Bible into German, so placing in the hands of his countrymen the weapon which he himself had used to defy the Church. Luther, however, was insistent on his own interpretation of the Bible, and when Lutheran churches sprang up, that interpretation was imposed upon the people in a spirit of narrow intolerance. Other reformers, such as Zwingli in Zurich, Switzerland, interpreted the Bible differently. Those who rejected the Roman Church never formed a united Protestant Church.

Civil War in Germany

Towards the end of Luther's life the Reformation in Germany came to be dominated by the German princes. Many of them saw benefits in throwing off the authority of the Pope. The German rulers became divided into Protestant and Catholic princes and civil war broke out in the year of Luther's death (1546), the Emperor Charles V being at the head of the Catholic forces. At last, by the Peace of Augsburg (1555), it was agreed to allow certain States to adopt the Lutheran religion and to disown the authority of the Pope. The religion of each state was to be decided by its ruler, a principle summed up in Latin as *cujus regio, ejus religio*. This principle expressed the fact that the princes were masters of the Church as well as of the State. The decision of Augsburg for a time averted further bloodshed, but it ended the religious unity of Germany and ultimately of Europe, and it destroyed the old Christendom with its bond of one Church.

Peace of Augsburg 1555

IV

THE REFORMATION IN ENGLAND
AND SCOTLAND

1. Henry VIII and the Pope

(i) *The Breach with Rome.*

HENRY VIII wrote to Leo X to say that 'ever since he knew of Luther's heresy in Germany, he had made it his study how to extirpate it'. Luther made an abusive reply: 'Damnable rottenness and worm that he is ... it is only right that I, in the cause of Christ, should bespatter his English Majesty with his own mud and filth.' But the Pope gave Henry the title of 'Defender of the Faith' (1521). Nevertheless, it was Henry VIII who began the movement known as the English Reformation, though in his time it was largely a political, not a religious, movement. The religious changes mostly came later. Henry VIII severed the connections between England and the Papacy.

Hostility to Papal power in England was no new thing. In the 14th century the Popes had resided in Avignon, not in Rome, and had been Frenchmen, not Italians, and the English had been inclined to suspect that they exercised their power in favour of the Kings of France. Hence the Kings and Parliament had shown themselves anxious to keep the control of the English Church in English hands. Both Edward III and Richard II had passed Statutes declaring papal appointments in England illegal and forbidding appeals to the papal court. On the other hand, ever since 1399, relations between English Kings and their subjects and the Popes had been particularly friendly. Yet after more than a century the old 14th century Statutes were used by Henry VIII to begin the English Reformation.

The origins of the English Reformation are inextricably mixed up with Henry VIII's matrimonial troubles. The immediate cause of the quarrel with the Pope was Henry's desire to divorce his wife,

Catherine of Aragon. When the question was first raised openly with the Pope in 1527 Henry and Catherine had been married eighteen years. During that time the queen had borne Henry seven children, but all had died in infancy except one, the Princess Mary, born in 1516 – and no woman had yet reigned in England. The last child was born in 1518; it was obvious by 1527 that Henry would die without a male heir unless he married again. Such a prospect was dangerous to the Tudor dynasty and might lead to another civil war. Besides, Henry very much wanted to marry again. He had conceived a violent passion for Anne Boleyn, a lady of the court. To make Anne Queen it was first necessary to get rid of Catherine. The death of all his male children troubled Henry's conscience and convinced him that his marriage with his brother's widow, apparently forbidden in the Old Testament Book of Leviticus, had offended God and was no true marriage.

Henry appealed to Pope Clement VII to annul the marriage. The Pope, however, was not in a position to offend the Spanish party. For Catherine was the aunt of the Emperor Charles V, whose troops had just occupied and sacked Rome, and the Pope was now the Emperor's prisoner. Charles V had become master of the Papacy at the moment that Henry VIII wanted his divorce problem solved. The most the Pope would do was to order the case to be tried before a Court, which included Cardinal Campeggio and Cardinal Wolsey, who was Papal Legate, that is, the Pope's representative in England. The Court opened at Blackfriars in May 1529. Two months later it was adjourned without coming to a decision. Then Campeggio left England. The next day a writ was issued against Wolsey for acting as Legate, although he had the king's licence to do so – but considerations of fairness never weighed with Henry VIII. The failure of the Court was followed by the fall of Wolsey, and by the summoning of Parliament (November 1529). Henry then began an attack on the papal power, relying on the English tradition, as old as the Conquest, of resistance to the claims of Rome.

The Legate's Court 1529

Fall and
death of
Wolsey
1529-30

Cardinal Wolsey was the first victim of the royal wrath. On the failure of the Court to pronounce judgement, he was dismissed from the king's service, and stripped of most of his wealth. The office of Chancellor was given to Sir Thomas More (1529). Next year Wolsey retired to his northern diocese, that of York. But while he was at Sheffield the King sent the Constable of the Tower to arrest him for treason. Wolsey, seeing that his death was intended, lost all hope. As he journeyed south he rapidly became ill, and had to be carried into Leicester Abbey. 'I am come to lay my bones among you', he said to the monks; and that night he died (1530). Among his last words was the tragic cry: 'If I had served God as diligently as I have done the king, He would not have given me over in my grey hairs'; and that cry truly reveals the spirit of Henry VIII's Monarchy. Yet Wolsey had long been the willing agent of that authoritarian Monarchy. 'He was feared by all,' wrote Erasmus; 'he was loved by few – I may say by nobody.'

The
Reformation
Parliament
1529-36

Meanwhile the famous 'Reformation Parliament' (1529-36) proceeded to do the king's will. As soon as it met in November 1529, it at once attacked clerical abuses by forbidding the holding of more than one church office, and by regulating the fees (for wills, burials, and so on) payable to the clergy and to the church courts – whereupon the clergy cried that 'the Commons seek the goods, not the good, of the Church'. Next, Henry prosecuted the clergy for having acknowledged Wolsey as Papal Legate, for this was contrary to the old Statutes of Praemunire; he then declared all Church property confiscate. Then followed the 'Submission of the Clergy', by which they agreed to pay a large fine, and to recognize Henry as 'chief protector and supreme head of the Church and Clergy, so far as the law of Christ will allow' (1531). Henry hoped that his attacks on the English Church would bring the Pope 'to reason'. When the Pope continued to refuse annulment of the King's marriage, the King

Anti-Papal
Acts

went further. Parliament passed the Annates Act (1532), forbidding a bishop on his election to pay his first year's income to 'Our Holy Father the Pope', as was customary.

THOMAS CRANMER (1489-1556)
(1545 portrait by Gerlach Flicke)

The Pope, however, still took no step to annul the king's marriage, and Henry decided to proceed without the Pope. A chaplain of the Boleyn family, Thomas Cranmer, had been consulting the universities of Europe about the divorce; and Henry remarked that Cranmer had 'got the sow by the right ear'. Events then moved swiftly. Some time in January 1533 Henry was secretly married to Anne Boleyn; in March Cranmer was made Archbishop of Canterbury; in April the Archbishop's Court pronounced Henry's marriage to Catherine null and void; and in June the secret marriage was acknowledged and Anne was crowned Queen of England. That autumn she gave birth

Cranmer

Henry marries Anne 1533

to a daughter, the future Queen Elizabeth. The birth of this child, illegitimate in the eyes of Catholic Europe, was a great disappointment to her father, who had hoped for a male heir. So the future Queen was heralded into the world amid an almost universal chorus of disapproval.

The putting away of the blameless Catherine, together with the marriage to Anne, was of course a flagrant defiance of the Pope. Clement VII pronounced Henry's marriage to Catherine valid (1533), and then prepared a Bull of Excommunication against the king (published two years later). But Henry had tasted power and knew his own strength. He was confident that there would be no repetition of the papal triumph of the days of King John, for though his divorce and the break with Rome were unpopular, he was sure that he could overcome any opposition. Besides, Henry knew that neither the King of France nor the Emperor was prepared to risk an invasion of England at the papal bidding. Henry, therefore, calmly proceeded on his way.

It remained to complete the breach with the Papacy. After Anne's coronation, Parliament passed the Appeals Act (1533), forbidding all appeals by English clergy to Rome. Next year came a series of important Acts, designed to bind the Church in England fast to the Royal Supremacy. All bishops were to be 'elected' by the cathedral chapters; but the chapters were bound to elect, within twelve days, the person nominated by the king. All payments of money (including Peter's Pence) to Rome were forbidden; and the clergy were not to take any oath to 'the Bishop of Rome, otherwise called the Pope'. Further, by the Act of Succession (1534), Princess Mary was declared illegitimate and the Crown was vested in the heirs of Henry VIII and Anne Boleyn. All subjects were required to take the Oath to the Succession or be charged with high treason. Sir Thomas More and Bishop Fisher refused and were imprisoned. Then Parliament ordained in the famous Act of Supremacy (1534) that 'the king, our sovereign lord, his heirs and successors, kings of this realm, shall be

Excommunication of Henry 1533

Act of Succession 1534

Act of Supremacy 1534

taken, accepted and reputed the only supreme head in earth of the Church of England, called *Anglicana Ecclesia*'. Finally, a stern Treasons Act, of the same year, enacted that anyone who called the King a tyrant, heretic, infidel, or usurper, was liable to the death penalty. With the last session (1536) of the Reformation Parliament came the overthrow of the lesser monasteries.

Thus, during the seven years of the Reformation Parliament (1529-36), through the passing of the Acts of Annates, Appeals, and Supremacy, Henry VIII severed the age-long connection with Rome. The Pope's powers had mostly been taken over by the King; no longer were the clergy (in Henry's own words) 'but half our subjects'. This revolution certainly did not express the will of the nation at large, but it did not seem much to affect most people. Those it did affect, the clergy, were soon made aware of the consequences of resistance.

(ii) *The Triumph of Henry VIII.*

In 1534, the year that the Act of Supremacy was passed, the son of a Putney clothworker named Thomas Cromwell was made the king's secretary. Cromwell owed his promotion to his own abilities, which had earlier gained him a post in Wolsey's household. For the next six years (1534-40) this able man acted as one of the King's chief advisers and did his utmost to carry out his master's will. One of his main tasks was to investigate any opposition to the King's policies and to make an example of any opponents he discovered.

Thomas Cromwell 1534-40

The first victims of the regime were five courageous priests who were sent to their death (1535) for refusing to swear to the Acts of Succession and Supremacy. They were John Houghton, prior of the London Charterhouse, two other Carthusian priors, another monk, and John Hale, vicar of Isleworth. The next to suffer were two eminent men – More, the great scholar, and Fisher, the saintly bishop of Rochester, a friend of Erasmus and Catherine's

Execution of the Carthusian monks 1535

confessor. They were now brought to trial and condemned for treason.

Execution of Fisher

Fisher was the first to die. Henry's wrath was especially aroused against him, as the Pope had just made him a cardinal. 'What, is he still so lusty?' exclaimed the wrathful King, 'Well, let the Pope send him a hat when he will; but I will provide that when so ever it cometh, he shall wear it on his shoulders, for head he shall have none to set it on.' Fisher, an old man of nearly seventy, excited popular sympathy by his noble bearing at the end. On the morning of his execution he told his servant to remove the hair shirt which he usually wore, 'and instead thereof to lay him forth a clean white shirt and all the best apparel he had as cleanly bright as may be'. The servant asked him why he so commanded. 'Dost thou not mark', said the bishop, 'that this is our wedding day, and that it behoveth us therefore to use more cleanliness of the marriage?' After the execution the bishop's head was impaled on London Bridge. The next day the King attended a play in which His Majesty was represented as cutting off the heads of the clergy – a performance which greatly appealed to the royal sense of humour.

Trial of More

When More was first examined (1534), the Duke of Norfolk had reminded him of the danger in which he stood. 'The wrath of the prince,' said Norfolk, 'is death.' 'Is that all, my lord?' replied More. 'Then in good faith the difference between your grace and me is that I shall die to-day and you to-morrow.' Perhaps the duke remembered these words thirteen years later, when he awaited the executioner's axe. In July 1535 More was tried in Westminster Hall for 'traitorously attempting to deprive the king of his title of Supreme Head of the Church of England'. After he was condemned he spoke his mind openly to the Chancellor who presided. 'My lord, for one bishop of your opinion, I have a hundred saints of mine; and for one Parliament of yours, and God knows of what kind, I have all the general councils (of the church) for a thousand years.' A week later he was beheaded. 'Pluck up thy spirit, man,' he said to the executioner – for his own courage did not fail. As he knelt at the block, he moved aside his beard. 'Pity that should be cut', he said, 'that has not committed treason.' So, with a jest upon his lips, he died.

The execution of the Carthusian monks, of Cardinal Fisher, and of Sir Thomas More sent a thrill of horror throughout Christendom. These men, the first Catholic martyrs in England, had to choose between loyalty to the king and loyalty to their religion. They bravely chose the latter. None had tried to stir up opposition to the King. All were men of saintly reputation, but that is why they had to die. If men such as these were known to doubt the rightness of the King's policies, others might come to share them.

The year after More's execution the Queen, Anne Boleyn, went to her doom. She had failed in her main duty, which was to produce a male heir. She was accused of misconduct, tried, condemned, and executed (1536). Two days before her execution Cranmer pronounced her marriage to the king invalid, and on the day she died he gave Henry a special licence to marry again. The next day Henry was betrothed to a lady called Jane Seymour, and he married her within a fortnight. The disgusting haste of the whole proceedings throws a lurid light on his character. Jane Seymour, alone of Henry's Queens, fulfilled his hopes, for she gave him the desired heir, the future Edward VI (born 1537); but she survived the birth of her son by only twelve days.

Meanwhile Henry took a step which further increased his power and wealth. This was an attack on Church property, the dissolution of the monasteries (1535-9). Henry found three reasons for this step. First, some of the monks regretted the downfall of Papal authority in England, as the Carthusians had shown, and many were members of orders which were spread over Europe. The second reason was the great wealth of the monasteries, which was the result of the pious bequests of many centuries. The cry against monastic wealth had been raised previously in English history, particularly in the time of

Edward III and Richard II. Henry VIII was well aware that shortage of money was a serious limitation on his power and in 1538-40 he needed to improve the defences of the country against a possible attack from Francis I or Charles V, then enjoying a rare period of mutual friendship. The third reason for ending the monasteries was the reason given to Parliament: that the monks were neglecting their spiritual duties and failing to obey their Rule. There were over 800 religious houses in England, and no doubt there was some truth in this charge. Zealous churchmen had long known that all was not well with some of these ancient institutions. In Henry VII's reign the Oxford reformers had rebuked monkish follies, and Cardinal Morton had noted the 'incurable uselessness' of many of the smaller houses where the monks were idle and ignorant. Cardinal Wolsey had obtained a Papal Bull to visit the monasteries, and had begun to suppress some, intending to use their revenues for the benefit of education and the New Learning and to found new bishoprics. One of them, St. Frideswide's Priory at Oxford, he converted into Cardinal College (later Christ Church).

Cromwell's visitation
In 1535 Henry made Thomas Cromwell his Vicar-General, with power to visit any monastery in England. His agents hurried through England, visited most of the monasteries, and drew up reports. It has often been suggested that these reports were largely propaganda, designed simply to justify the dissolution of the monasteries that had already been decided upon. Yet even a propaganda exercise has to be convincing, which would hardly be the case if the visitors had simply made up all their evidence against the monasteries. Moreover, the quantity and variety of local detail in their reports indicate a certain conscientiousness on the visitors' part. The visitors were also willing to give monasteries a clean bill of health, as in many cases they did. To a modern reader, the reports are not so very damning: the vow of chastity, for example, was very widely observed. Contemporaries saw the matter differently: they expected very high standards among those who enjoyed large endowments and devoted their lives to religion.

That their inmates could plausibly be accused of *manifest sin, vicious, carnal and abominable living* must have helped to damn the smaller monasteries in the eyes of MPs, who in 1536 passed an Act dissolving about 250 of the lesser monasteries of England.

In dissolving the smaller monasteries first, Henry had cautiously tested his power. But his violent measures had (by 1536) caused grave discontent, especially in the north. His wholesale destruction of the smaller monasteries was followed by two popular uprisings. The first occurred in Lincolnshire, where the rebels accepted a pardon and dispersed after the arrival of a military force under the Duke of Suffolk. The second rising, in Yorkshire, and the far north, known as the Pilgrimage of Grace, was much more serious (1536). In the barren north, where towns were few and far between, the monks were still popular. In Yorkshire they had been the only people to dispense hospitality to the wandering beggar and the ordinary traveller. The work of the Cistercians, too, as sheep-farmers, was a benefit to a country where agriculture was difficult; and it was feared that the dissolution of the larger abbeys (like Fountains) was only a matter of time.

A lawyer called Robert Aske mustered the rebels on Skipworth Moor, and then took possession of York; the expelled monks were restored to their monasteries. The King then sent the Duke of Norfolk to Yorkshire, but when the latter reached Doncaster he found the rebels 30,000 strong and too formidable to risk a battle. So he adopted the usual expedient in such cases – a general promise of pardon if the rebels would submit, and this was successful for the time being. But a further outbreak (1537) gave the King an excuse to act with a ferocity congenial to his temper. 'You shall in any wise,' he wrote to his agents, 'cause such dreadful execution to be done upon a good number of the inhabitants of every town, village and hamlet … as well by the hanging of them up in trees or by the quartering of them, and the setting of their heads and quarters in every town great or small, as they may be a fearful spectacle to others hereafter that they would practise any like matter.' The leaders and no

Lesser monasteries dissolved 1536

Pilgrimage of Grace 1536

less than twelve abbots were hanged for their part in the rebellion. That was the end of the Pilgrimage of Grace.

The following year the famous shrine of Becket at Canterbury was attacked. Thomas Becket was declared (April 1538) 'a false saint and a traitor to the Supreme Head of the Church'; his bones were burnt, his shrine pillaged and its offerings confiscated – and thus Henry VIII in his own way showed that he had won the battle that Henry II had lost.

Dissolution of the larger abbeys 1539

Then Henry was ready to turn his attention to the greater monasteries, although Parliament had saved them earlier because of their monks' good conduct. Cromwell and his agents now (1539) began a persecution of the abbots: many were induced to surrender their abbeys to the king; others could only be reduced by methods of terror. The Abbots of Reading and Colchester were tried for treason; the Abbot of Glastonbury for felony. All three were executed. The methods of Cromwell are well shown in some notes left in his own handwriting: 'To see that the evidence be well sorted and the indictments well drawn against the said abbots. The Abbot of Reading to be sent down to be tried and executed at Reading with his complices. The Abbot of Glaston to be tried at Glaston, and also executed there with his complices.' The last Abbot of Glastonbury, a pious, venerable man beloved in the countryside, was executed with two of his brethren on Glastonbury Tor, after a mock trial (November 1539); the quarters of his dismembered body were displayed in four Somerset towns. These ferocities had the desired effect: many less brave spirits gave in, and soon there were no monasteries left.

Monastic wealth

The dissolution of the religious houses was the greatest revolution in the ownership of land in England since the Norman Conquest. The monastic income of perhaps about £200,000 a year has been variously estimated at between one-fifth and one-third of the total rental of England. This newly acquired wealth the king might have used in developing public works, such as education. Some of it was spent in re-building the Navy and fortifying the coast; but the King sold off most of the lands in order to fund his wars with France and Scotland in the 1540s. The newly landed henceforth had a strong interest in maintaining the changes of Henry's reign. The 'Abbey' where the descendants or successors of these Tudor families now live is a name to be found in many an English village. But sad indeed was the fate of the original buildings. Some, like the great church at Tewkesbury, have been preserved in the form of parish churches; others have been partly preserved to form cathedrals.[11] But the greater number were ruthlessly destroyed by their new possessors, their roofs despoiled for the valuable lead, their walls made quarries for new buildings, their treasures scattered, and their ruins left desolate. Whatever defence may be made for the suppression of the monastic orders, no excuse can be offered for this orgy of destruction, which deprived England of some of her noblest monuments.

Ruin of the abbeys

It is probable that at least 15,000 persons were cast adrift. These people went to swell the already large number of the unemployed, for whom Tudor statesmanship could find no better relief than the savage punishments inflicted on thieves and vagabonds. Some of the monks were given jobs as parish priests or pensioned by the Government, but the pensions were not always paid; the occupants of the lesser houses fared worse than those of the greater. The hospitality which the monks had always given to the poor was now removed. There was nothing to take its place, and some monks and nuns joined the ranks of those who had formerly subsisted on their charity. Many gaps[12] were left in national life, for the abbeys (said

---

[11] The abbeys of Peterborough, Gloucester, Bristol, Chester, and Oxford were made into the seats of new bishoprics by Henry VIII, and these abbey churches were thus preserved in the form of cathedrals. Westminster Abbey was also made the seat of a bishopric; and though the bishopric was afterwards suppressed, the abbey was given to St. Paul's Cathedral, and so happily preserved.

[12] Thirty-one abbots now disappeared from the House of Lords, and for the first time the lay lords outnumbered the spiritual lords.

Aske) 'were one of the beauties of this realm to all men and strangers passing through the same; all gentlemen much succoured in their needs with money, and in nunneries their daughters brought up in virtue. And such abbeys as were near the danger of seabanks were great maintainers of sea-walls and dykes, builders of bridges and highways, and such other things for the commonwealth.'

(iii) *Conflicting Parties.*

Henry VIII and the Reformers

When he had enforced the Act of Supremacy, destroyed the monasteries, and sent the chief supporters of the Pope's authority to their death, Henry VIII's Reformation was completed. He had achieved the fusion of Church and State under one head, the Sovereign, as nearly as it was possible for any man to do so. But Henry was no Lutheran. He had no more sympathy with the reformers in doctrine now than he had when he wrote his book against Luther, and English Lutherans had been burnt at the stake. The King would permit no change in the traditional form of Catholic worship. But if Henry was untouched by the ideas of the German Reformers, there were some people in England, including Archbishop Cranmer, who were attracted by them. One of the main changes which Luther made in Germany was the translation of the Bible into his native tongue. And Cranmer and Cromwell were eventually able to persuade the king to make one concession to the reforming spirit, and allow an English Bible to be published.

Tyndale's Bible

The only English Bible circulating (secretly) in the early 16th century had been produced by 14th century heretics and had never been printed. In the 1520s a young Oxford scholar named William Tyndale translated most of the Bible afresh into English from the original Greek and Hebrew. 'If God spare my life,' he said to some ignorant clergymen to whom he talked, 'I will cause a boy that driveth a plough shall know more of the Scriptures than thou dost.' Tyndale travelled in Germany, heard Luther preach, and became a Protestant. His great translation, one of the noblest works in English, was later made the basis of the Authorized Version of James I's reign. But under Henry VIII it was not allowed into England, and Tyndale himself was soon afterwards burnt as a heretic in the Netherlands at the behest of Sir Thomas More. But since, in spite of prohibitions, Tyndale's Bible was smuggled into England and sold there, it was decided to issue an official translation, made by 'great, learned and Catholic persons'. Under Cromwell's patronage, Miles Coverdale produced a revised translation, which, known as the Great Bible, was issued with the king's authority in 1539 and ordered to be used in all churches. At the end of the reign a Litany also appeared in English.

The Great Bible 1539

In doctrinal matters Henry continued to be rigidly orthodox. The Act of Six Articles was passed by Parliament (1539), making it punishable by burning to deny the Catholic doctrine of the eucharist. In addition, priests were to remain unmarried, laymen were to continue to receive only the bread at communion, and the necessity of confession to a priest was reaffirmed. This Act became known as the 'Whip with six strings'; Cranmer shook in his shoes and packed off his wife and children to Germany. In the same year, six men were executed at the same time and place: three were priests hanged for denying the Royal Supremacy; three were Protestant heretics, condemned under the Act of Six Articles. In this same year, too, a man was hanged in London for eating meat on a Friday.

Six Articles 1539

Meanwhile Thomas Cromwell, fresh from his triumphs over monks, was arranging to ally Henry with the Protestant princes of Germany, as a safeguard against the possibility that the Catholic monarchs Francis I and Charles V might attack England. He hastily negotiated a marriage between the King and Anne, sister of the Duke of Cleves (on the Rhine).

Anne of Cleves

But when this Lutheran princess arrived in England, Henry had changed his mind about the German alliance. He also took an immediate dislike to Anne; he married her early in 1540, but looked about for an excuse to divorce her as soon as possible. His wrath fell on Cromwell, who was also accused of protecting Protestants. He

Execution of
Cromwell
1540 was arrested for treason in June, sentenced without trial and condemned unheard, and finally beheaded in July. He had been Henry VIII's supremely efficient agent, who, as usual with Henry's ministers, was blamed for the less creditable aspects of the King's rule, especially the savage punishments meted out to critics. While Cromwell held sway, 'men felt', said Erasmus, 'as though a scorpion lay sleeping beneath every stone'.

Henry's
last days   In the same year Henry found means for divorcing Anne of Cleves, and, partly to mark his disapproval of the reforming party, he next married Catherine Howard, niece of the Duke of Norfolk, who was the leader of the orthodox nobles. But Catherine committed adultery and so suffered the same fate as her cousin Anne Boleyn. In 1543 Henry married his sixth and last wife, Catherine Parr,[13] who had already outlived two husbands, and was destined to outlive the king. Her influence, in so far as she dared assert it, was exerted on the side of the Protestant-inclined reformers, and in Henry's last years the Norfolk (Catholic) party suffered a decline. In December 1546 Norfolk and his son, the Earl of Surrey, were suddenly arrested on a charge of treason. In the New Year, however, the king became Death of
Henry VIII
1547 very ill; on the 15th of January Surrey was beheaded; on the 27th Norfolk was sentenced to death; on the 28th the king died, so that Norfolk was saved in the nick of time.

It remains to note how Henry VIII, like his ancestor Edward I, asserted his influence in all parts of the British Isles. After the Pilgrimage of Grace, he reorganized the Council of the North and ceased to rely on the old noble families such as the Percies to keep that

---

[13] Note the *political aspect* of Henry's marriages:
1. Catherine of Aragon (1509), Spanish alliance.
2. Anne Boleyn, and 3. Jane Seymour, Breach with Rome.
4. Anne of Cleves, Alliance with German Protestants.
5. Catherine Howard, Reaction in favour of English Catholics.
6. Catherine Parr, English Protestant party more in favour.

remote area in order. And, as befitted a king of Welsh descent, he finally incorporated Wales into England. He increased the power of the Council of Wales and ended the special judicial arrangements of the border areas. From this time on all of Wales was divided into counties, just like England, and was governed in the same way, while Welsh counties and towns henceforth sent their representatives to the English parliament. Thus Wales, without sacrificing its language and culture, became a part of England. 'A better people to govern,' it was said, 'and better subjects of their sovereign, Europe holdeth not.' Wales

Henry VIII also attempted the reorganization of Ireland. After his breach with the Pope, he declared himself King (instead of Lord) of Ireland. He had earlier suppressed a rebellion by the Earl of Kildare, who was executed for treason at Tyburn in 1537. Thereafter Henry tried to Anglicize Ireland. The Irish were ordered to speak English and wear English clothes. Irish chiefs were enriched with Irish abbeys and lands, as a bribe to induce them to accept the Royal Supremacy over the Irish Church and to attend the Irish Parliament. Ireland was to be Henry's second kingdom, modelled on his first one, England. Ireland

Finally, Henry VIII hoped to unite the Crowns of England and Scotland. After he had been involved in a war with his nephew, James V, who died shortly after the defeat of his forces at Solway Moss in 1542, Henry proposed to marry his young heir, Prince Edward, to the Scottish baby princess, Mary Stuart. He seemed to think that the best way to bring about this marriage was to strike fear into the Scots by sending the Earl of Hertford with an army to burn Edinburgh – which was done in 1544. The Scots fell back on the old French alliance, and Henry, who had been at peace with France for nearly twenty years, declared war on his old rival Francis I (1543). The war resulted in Henry's capture of the port of Boulogne, but there was a serious invasion scare in 1545, nothing whatever was achieved in Scotland and the King incurred huge costs. Shortly after the conclusion of peace between France and England, both Francis and Henry died. Scotland

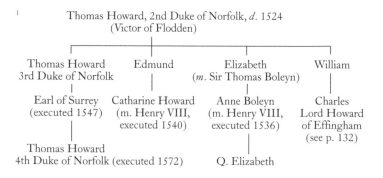

Thomas Howard, 2nd Duke of Norfolk, *d*. 1524
(Victor of Flodden)

Thomas Howard
3rd Duke of Norfolk

Earl of Surrey
(executed 1547)

Thomas Howard
4th Duke of Norfolk (executed 1572)

Edmund

Catharine Howard
(m. Henry VIII,
executed 1540)

Elizabeth
(*m*. Sir Thomas Boleyn)

Anne Boleyn
(m. Henry VIII,
executed 1536)

Q. Elizabeth

William

Charles
Lord Howard
of Effingham
(see p. 132)

Henry VIII
and
Parliament

Henry VIII had consolidated the Tudor Monarchy, the foundations of which his father had laid. Henry had risked internal unrest and foreign attack by divorcing a popular Queen and breaking with the Papacy, but the Monarchy had proved strong enough to survive every threat. At Henry's death the King was master of the national Church and had strengthened his control of the nobility in general and formerly lawless areas like the North and Wales in particular. Parliament had become more important too. In carrying through the break with Rome, it had dealt with more important matters than ever before. Henceforth, there was no law higher than the laws passed by Parliament, not even the laws of the Church. The House of Commons began to increase its powers. For example, it was in 1523 that the Speaker (Sir Thomas More) first claimed for the Commons that right to 'freedom of speech' which was later to be regarded as one of the House's most valued privileges.

'I seem to see in him,' the great Victorian historian Stubbs wrote of Henry VIII, 'a grand, gross figure, very far removed from ordinary human sympathies …. He was a man who might have been very great, and could under no circumstances be accounted less than great, but who would have been infinitely greater, and better, and more fortunate, if he could have lived for his people, and not for himself.'[14] Henry's greatness was perhaps least apparent in his final years. Physically, he became a monstrous, corpulent figure, and he left to his son an unresolved problem in Scotland, uncertain relations with France, which was itching to recover Boulogne, and an empty treasury.

2. Edward VI and the Protestant Religion

(i) *Protector Somerset.*

Henry VIII had been empowered by Parliament to regulate the succession to the Crown by his will. He left it first to his only son, Edward, then (if Edward had no heir) to his daughters Mary and Elizabeth; if neither Mary nor Elizabeth had heirs, the Crown was to go to the descendants of his younger sister Mary, Duchess of Suffolk. This will was carried out so far as the children of Henry VIII were concerned: the provision with regard to the Suffolk line was disregarded and the descendants of his elder sister, Margaret Queen of Scotland, inherited after Elizabeth.

Will of Henry VIII

Edward VI was a precocious boy, not quite ten years old. The strong hand of the late king had just been able to control the two parties (those in favour and those against more religious change) who had struggled for supremacy during his last ten years. Henry had hoped there would be no abrupt change of policy at his death. But with the new king a minor, the factions broke loose, as they had done when Henry VI was a minor. The government was in the hands of a council of ministers nominated by the late king, of whom the chief was the Protestant-inclined Edward Seymour, Earl of Hertford, shortly afterwards created Duke of Somerset. He was the King's uncle, and the Council allowed him to assume the office of Protector (1547-9).

Edward VI 1547-53

Somerset's first concern was with Scotland. Like the late King, he was strongly in favour of the union of the two countries, and at once followed up the question of the marriage of the two young monarchs,

Somerset

Scotland

---

[14] Stubbs, *Lectures on Medieval and Modern History*, xii.

Battle of
Pinkie 1547

Edward VI and Mary Queen of Scots. This scheme was intended to end the age-long conflict between the two kingdoms. The Protector tried persuasion and failed, and then resorted to force. He invaded Scotland; and, with the help of Italian musketeers, he won a crushing but fruitless victory at Pinkie Clough (1547). Somerset used his victory with moderation, for he still hoped for a settlement. But the Scots would have none of the English alliance, and they shipped their young Queen off to France, where she was betrothed to the Dauphin Francis, the King's heir.

Policy of
Somerset

The first Parliament of the reign was summoned that autumn, on the Protector's return from the North. Its chief work was to pass laws which showed that the reformers, headed by Somerset, intended to abandon Henry VIII's religious position. At Somerset's bidding an Act was passed repealing the late King's treason and heresy laws (including the Act of Six Articles). The Act went farther; it also repealed the Statute '*De Heretico Comburendo*', under which heretics, from the days of Henry IV onwards, had been put to death by burning. With the help of these laws Somerset meant to use his power to modify Henry VIII's harsh system of rule. During the three years he was in power no political prisoner was tortured in the Tower, and no restrictions were placed on the activity of the printing-press or the publication of the Scriptures. It was not this first experiment in mercy that caused the Protector's fall. It was when he went farther, and seemed to champion peasants against rich men, that he found stern reality too much for him.

One effect of the repeal of the heresy laws was immediately felt. England was soon invaded by a host of foreign preachers: reformers from Geneva, Zurich, and Germany, as well as Italians, Poles, Flemings, and Frenchmen – all ready to propagate their views. This situation had its disadvantages, and Englishmen were confused by a babel of strange voices preaching strange doctrines.

The Protector was not rash enough to go as far as some of the Protestant zealots wished in breaking away from Catholic practices.

EDWARD VI (1537-1553, REIGN: 1547-1553)
(Portrait c. 1550 by William Scrots)

However, it was felt desirable to introduce a form of worship in the English language. The result was the drawing up of the beautiful English liturgy known as the First Prayer Book of Edward VI (1549) – one of the greatest treasures in the English language. It was largely the work of Cranmer. With very few changes it was a translation from the old Latin service-books, and it showed few traces of the teaching of the German reformers who were now crowding into England to escape the triumphant Charles V. In order to enforce its uniform use all over the land, Parliament passed the First Act of Uniformity (1549). The use of the new service, however, provoked much discontent, especially in Devon and Cornwall, where there was a rebellion. To Catholics, above all in Ireland, Wales, and Cornwall, the new Prayer Book was, as the Cornishmen said, 'but like a Christmas game, and we Cornishmen (whereof

First Prayer Book of Edward VI 1549

First Act of Uniformity 1549

certain of us understand not English) utterly refuse this new English'.

The Enclosure evil

Meanwhile the Protector turned his attention to one of the crying evils of the time – the results of the 'enclosures', which had been slowly going on ever since the Black Death. Sir Thomas More had complained of the misery caused by the enclosing of arable land for sheep-farming. What More and others complained of was: (i) the turning of arable land into pasture and its enclosure by a hedge, which reduced the demand for labour; (ii) the take-over by private owners of the common lands of villages, which deprived the poor of grazing and other rights and so made them poorer; and (iii) the consolidation of two or more peasant holdings into one farm and its fencing off, which replaced two peasants by one richer one. Hence, it was believed, enclosure was a chief cause of the growing numbers of the poor in rural England. Many writers of the time believed that enclosure was a great social evil. Hugh Latimer, Bishop of Worcester, preaching before the king, told him that

> 'the honest ploughman is in Christ equal with the greatest prince that is. Let them, therefore, have sufficient to maintain them and to find them their necessaries. They must have cattle, as horses to draw their plough, and for carriage of things to the markets, and kine for their milk and cheese which they must live upon and pay their rents. These cattle must have pasture, and pasture they cannot have if the land be taken in and *enclosed* from them. Therefore, for God's love restore sufficient unto them, and search no more for the cause of rebellion.'

Latimer was himself the son of a small but prosperous yeoman farmer, whereas he who 'now hath the farm is not able to do anything for his prince, for himself, nor for his children, or give a cup of drink to the poor'.

For this evil, Somerset tried to devise a remedy. He set up a Commission (1548) to inquire into the spread of enclosures, and prepared measures to check it. But he soon found that the gentry, whose representatives sat in Parliament and who dominated their local communities, were too strong for him. By all means in their power they hindered the work of the Commissioners.

But while the gentry were holding up the Protector's good work, the peasantry rose in rebellion against the social evils of the time. The chief of these were enclosures, and the debasing of the coinage – begun by the late King and continued after him – which increased prices and caused distress because wages tended to lag behind them. The revolt began in the west, spread through Gloucester and Dorset to most of the Midland shires, and came to a head in Norfolk. There Robert Ket, a prosperous farmer and tanner, who had taken the side of the oppressed peasantry, raised a rebel army and captured Norwich. In the midst of the confusion the French – urged by the Scots who were anxious to avenge Pinkie – seized this opportune moment to declare war on England (August 1549). The Council chose John Dudley, Earl of Warwick, to put down Ket's rebellion, and he defeated the rebels near Mousehold Heath, outside Norwich.

Ket's Rebellion 1549

Somerset agreed that the rebels must be put down, but he was accused of having encouraged revolt by his original sympathy for the poor and the Council was determined on his fall. He was deposed from his office as Protector, arrested, and sent to the Tower (October 1549).

Somerset deposed

Somerset occupies an important place in English history as the first Protestant ruler of this country. A major blot on his character was his greediness in profiting by the destruction of the monasteries and other Church property.[15] However, what destroyed him was the arrogant style of his rule, which offended the other Councillors and led him to ignore his need to carry them with him, and the lack of realism he showed in his Scottish and social policies.

---

[15] Out of his ill-gotten gains he built Somerset House (not the present building, which dates from the end of the eighteenth century).

(ii) *Northumberland.*

John Dudley   The Earl of Warwick was now the virtual head of the Government. He was the son of Dudley, Henry VII's unpopular minister whom Henry VIII had put to death. He never took the title of Protector, but he had great influence over the young king, and ruled in his name. At first he was reconciled to Somerset, who was released from the Tower and re-admitted to the Council. But the Catholic members of the Council were expelled, and Warwick prepared to launch out on a vigorous policy of religious reform.

Dissolution of the chantries and guilds   Throughout Edward VI's reign, and especially under Warwick, there occurred what has been called the 'Great Pillage of the Church', when, in Bishop Latimer's words, 'thousands became Gospellers for the sake of the Church lands'. The chantries, the guilds, the churches themselves were all attacked. The chantries were chapels where Masses for the souls of the departed were said, a practice to which Protestants were opposed. Some chantry priests had also kept schools, and had thus performed a valuable service to the community. Similarly, the guilds had been for centuries intimately connected, as benefit or friendly societies, with the daily life of the people; and they suffered a severe blow when the portion of their property devoted to religious uses was confiscated (from 1547). Many of the craft guilds survived, including the powerful City Guilds of London, which remain to this day. But the guild system of industry was already giving way to more competitive and modern methods.

Spoilation of the churches   Still more upsetting to the ordinary folk of village and town was the spoiling of the churches themselves. Many were robbed of their rich vestments, their jewels of gold and silver, crosses, candlesticks, and chalices, and even of their lead roofing. The pictures on the walls, by which the Church had instructed simple folk in their faith, were blotted out, and the churches were white-limed and painted with texts. The images (which to Protestant zealots were idolatrous) were defaced and the rood-screens pulled down. Thus, many things of beauty and solace were wantonly destroyed. When the chantries and religious guilds were suppressed, the proceeds were supposed to be used for building schools and relieving the poor. Some old schools were re-founded and became known as King Edward VI's Grammar Schools. But only a comparatively small part of the spoils was in fact used for the general good of the community. The rest went to replenish the impoverished Treasury, and the lands were sold to the same sort of wealthy people who had purchased the monastic lands. Moreover, most of the Church festivals were done away with, and this meant that the workers lost the many holidays – 'holy days' on which work was forbidden – that had relieved their long hours of labour for centuries.

In foreign affairs the new government's policies were dictated by its lack of money. Peace was made with France and Scotland, but Boulogne was surrendered for half the sum which the French had promised, and the English strongholds in Scotland were given up without compensation. The French were left masters of Scotland, with the Dauphin wedded to the Scottish Queen, and Henry II of France boasting that he ruled three realms – France, Scotland, and England.

It was natural that the men who resented the reversal of the Protector's policy should gather round the fallen minister. But Warwick, whom Edward created Duke of Northumberland in 1551, decided that he was now strong enough to strike down his old rival. Somerset was arrested and tried on a charge of high treason, 'the more pitied by the people for the known hatred of Northumberland against him'. He was found guilty and executed (January 1552).

Execution of Somerset 1552

Northumberland pursued an extreme policy of Protestant reform, partly in order to please the Protestants, and partly owing to the need for money. Bishops who objected were deprived of their sees, and among these were Bonner, bishop of London, and Gardiner, bishop of Winchester. Revenues from the sees of deposed bishops, chantry lands, Church plate – all were used to augment the Government's resources. Edward VI himself was a sincere and ardent reformer, and

Second
Prayer Book
1552
greatly interested in advancing the new doctrines. This was one of the means Northumberland used to maintain his hold over Edward's mind. In 1552 a Second Prayer Book was forced on the people. Very different from the First, it was drawn up under the influence of German and Swiss Protestants. In it the Communion Service is no longer a translated Mass, but a very different service. Its use was enforced by a Second Act of Uniformity. The following year the Forty-two Articles, defining the doctrine of the English Protestant Church, were drawn up by Cranmer, and all clergymen had to subscribe to this summary of doctrines. At the same time the destruction of Church property went on apace.

The government was extremely unpopular in the country. Fearing risings, and no longer possessing enough money to employ foreign mercenaries, as Somerset had, Northumberland appointed various local gentlemen lords lieutenant, commissioned to raise troops against the King's enemies. Yet the rule of Northumberland mainly depended on the continuance of the King's favour. His influence over Edward showed no signs of abating, but, unfortunately for him, the King succumbed to tuberculosis, and it soon became obvious that he had not much longer to live. In 1553 Edward was persuaded to make a will, by which he 'devised' the Crown to his second cousin, Lady Jane Grey, a daughter of the Duchess of Suffolk, who was herself a granddaughter of Henry VII.[16] The claims of Lady Jane, as compared with those of the Princesses Mary and Elizabeth, or of the Scottish line, were obviously weak. But Northumberland was determined that the Catholic Mary, Edward's elder sister and real heiress, should not succeed. In order to strengthen his own position he married Lady Jane to one of his sons, Guildford Dudley, and then forced the Council to agree to the arbitrary choice of Jane as the next sovereign of England.

In July 1553 Edward VI died, exclaiming (he was only fifteen), 'Oh, my Lord God, deliver this country from papistry, and defend Thy true religion.' Northumberland at once had his daughter-in-law proclaimed Queen. He had failed, however, to seize the Princess Mary, who escaped to rally her adherents in the eastern counties, where the memory of Northumberland's suppression of Ket's rebellion was still vivid. Northumberland set off with an army to confront her, but the Council in London, in his absence, repudiated 'Queen Jane' and declared for Queen Mary. Then he knew that the game was up and surrendered. Mary entered London amid the rejoicings of a city which was delighted to welcome a true Tudor as sovereign. Lady Jane Grey

So ended for a time the attempt to make England Protestant. Many of the reformers, like Bishop Latimer of Worcester, were conscientious and able men, anxious to build up a Protestant Church in England. But in Edward's reign Protestantism had become associated with an attack on local church property which was bitterly resented. In these circumstances, people stopped giving to their churches, young men ceased to enter the priesthood and attendance at services fell off.

HENRY VII

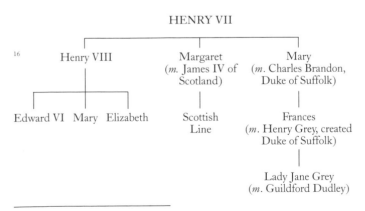

16

Diagram of family tree.

3. Mary and the Catholic Revival

Mary 1553-8 Queen Mary, the first woman to rule England as Queen in her own right, was thirty-seven years old. The daughter of Catherine of Aragon, she looked back on a life passed, from girlhood, in bitter humiliation. Her father's cruel treatment of her mother, and the persecution which she herself had suffered, first from her father and then from Northumberland, were memories which had burnt themselves deep into her soul. She was a woman of limited understanding, but of deep piety and sincerity. Her main object, now that she had become Queen, was to restore, to its full medieval power, the Church to whose authority she herself gave an unquestioning obedience. But if she dreamt of restoring Church property, Mary little knew the character of the men who had come into possession of it under Henry VIII and Edward VI.

Execution of North-umberland The reign began in a glow of popularity, which the Queen did not tarnish by undue severity. Northumberland was executed as a traitor, Lady Jane and her husband were sent to the Tower, but most of those implicated in the duke's plot were pardoned.

Mary's next action was to deprive Archbishop Cranmer and the leading Protestant bishops – Latimer, Hooper, and Ridley – of their sees. They were all sent to the Tower. At the same time Gardiner and Bonner were restored as bishops of Winchester and London. Mary's first Parliament was then summoned and persuaded to repeal the Act of Uniformity. Meanwhile many in the country were alarmed by the announcement of the Queen's intention to marry Philip of Habsburg, the son of her cousin, the Emperor Charles V.

But Mary's heart was set on this marriage, for it represented the reversal of English policy from the time of her mother's divorce. She proceeded with her plan, regardless of opposition. Her mission was to bring back England to the Catholic fold, and she saw in the Spanish alliance a means to that end. Moreover, she believed that she could rally her subjects to her support.

MARY I (1516-1558, REIGN 1553-1558)
(1554 portrait by Anthonis Mor.)

In 1554 a revolt broke out in Kent, led by Sir Thomas Wyatt, a prominent Kentish gentleman. The object of the rising was to dethrone Mary in favour of her sister Elizabeth, who was to be married to Edward Courtenay, a great-grandson of Edward IV. But Courtenay himself betrayed the plot to Mary's ministers, and though an army sent against Wyatt deserted, the Londoners heeded the Queen's courageous appeal to them and refused to let the rebels into the city. Wyatt was forced to lay down his arms. Elizabeth's life was at this time in considerable danger, for the imperial ambassador urged her execution. She was sent to the Tower for some months, and was only with difficulty restored to the Queen's good graces. Many executions followed the suppression of Wyatt's rebellion. Among the victims were the innocent Lady Jane Grey, her husband, Guildford Dudley, and her father, the Duke of Suffolk (1554).

Wyatt's rebellion 1554

The failure of Wyatt's rising enabled the Queen to proceed with

her double scheme – the Spanish marriage and the restoration of the papal authority. Philip of Spain landed in England in the summer of 1554; he was married to Mary by Gardiner in Winchester Cathedral with full Catholic ritual. Another and no less important visitor arrived soon after the marriage; this was Cardinal Pole,[17] made Papal Legate to England, and entrusted with the mission of reconciling England with the Pope. At a solemn session of Parliament, in the presence of the Queen, who stood weeping for joy, Cardinal Pole absolved the English nation and re-admitted it to the union of the Catholic

Church. 'Today,' some said, 'we are born again.' Parliament then repealed the Act of Supremacy and the rest of the anti-papal laws of Henry VIII. But neither Queen nor cardinal could persuade Parliament to restore the spoils of the monasteries, chantries, or guilds. The queen told them: 'I value the peace of my conscience more than ten such crowns as that of England.' But the families who had shared in the plunder held fast to their lands; indeed, Parliament had not agreed to Pole's coming to England until the Queen had promised not to restore the Church lands.

This same Parliament re-enacted the Statute '*De Heretico Comburendo*', which Somerset had repealed. The next year (1555) saw the beginning of the persecution – the burning of the Protestant martyrs. The descriptions of their deaths in the paragraphs below were written by the Protestant John Foxe in his *Book of Martyrs*, which became, after its publication in England in 1563, the most widely read book but for the Bible in the country. Thanks to him, Mary's

---

[17] Cardinal Pole was a member of a singularly unfortunate family. He was a grandson of George, Duke of Clarence, who had been murdered in the Tower by order of his brother, Edward IV. Pole's uncle, Clarence's son Warwick, was the innocent victim of Henry VII's cruelty (1499). In the next reign the Pole family was ruined; the Cardinal's elder brother, Lord Montague, was executed in 1539, while two years later his mother, Lady Salisbury, who was over 70 years of age, was also sacrificed to the whim of Henry VIII.

reign acquired an evil reputation which it has never lost. But, severe as the persecution was, this brief phase cannot compare with the terror which some other European countries endured – for example, the earlier crusade against Jews and Moors in Spain under Mary's maternal grandparents, or the later burning and slaughtering of Protestants under her husband's rule in the Netherlands. And, whatever the cruelties of Henry VIII and Mary, England was at least spared the horrors of a religious war.

The Marian Persecution (1555-8) continued for the rest of the reign. The first to suffer was John Rogers, who was so acclaimed by the spectators that 'it seemed as though he were being taken to his wedding'. Altogether about 300 persons of both sexes were burnt to death during these three years; most of them were obscure people up and down the country, though many suffered in London at Smithfield. The best known victims were the Protestant bishops. Bishop Hooper suffered at Gloucester; Bishops Latimer and Ridley at Oxford, where they were put to death in the presence of the Vice-Chancellor. 'Be of good comfort, Master Ridley,' said Latimer, as the fire was lit, 'Play the man; we shall this day light such a candle, by God's grace, in England, as I trust shall never be put out.' Latimer and Ridley

Thomas Cranmer, formerly Archbishop of Canterbury, was also burnt at Oxford (1556). He recanted his Protestant opinions after he was sentenced to death, but even then the Queen refused to spare his life. On the day of his execution a sermon was preached in St. Mary's Church, at the conclusion of which Cranmer was expected once more to deny his former opinions. But suddenly he refused to do so; instead he said: Martyrdom of Cranmer 1556

'Now here I renounce and refuse, as things written with my hand contrary to the truth which I thought in my heart, and written for fear of death, ... all such papers as I have signed with my hand since my degradation, wherein I have written

91

many things untrue. And forasmuch as my hand offended, my hand shall first be punished for it; for when I come to the fire, it shall be first burned. As for the Pope, I refuse him, as Christ's enemy and Antichrist, with all his false doctrine.'

But when his opponents heard him speak thus, they began to cry out: 'Stop the heretic's mouth and take him away.' So he was brought to the fire. 'And when the wood was kindled (says an old account) and the fire began to burn he put his right hand into the flame, which he held so steadfast that all men might see his hand burned before his body was touched. His eyes were lifted up to heaven, and oftentimes he repeated: "This unworthy right hand"; and using often the words, *"Lord Jesus, receive my spirit"*, in the greatness of the flame, he gave up the ghost.' There are many faults to be found in Thomas Cranmer, but in the face of that last heroic gesture, criticism may be silent.

So perished the Protestant martyrs, in the same spirit in which More and Fisher, and others less well known, had died for the Catholic faith. But, in spite of, or because of, the burning of Protestants, the Queen could not stamp out the Protestant religion in England. Before she came to the throne it was regarded with mixed feelings; now it was sealed with the blood of martyrs. 'The burning of the archbishop hath burned the Pope out of the land for ever and ever', predicted a peasant woman of the time. And such impartial observers as the Imperial and French ambassadors, Catholics though they were, were shocked by the burnings, while Philip warned Mary that she was proceeding at too great a pace. But nothing could check the fanatical woman, whose own sad life was now drawing to a close. She was disappointed in the hope of an heir, and began to feel with terrible foreboding that both her husband and her people were waiting for her to die. Philip left England in 1555; Mary waited month after month for his return. In 1557 he came back on a brief visit. He was now King of Spain, for his father, Charles V, had abdicated the throne. His mission was to embroil England in a war with France. He succeeded in his object, and then returned to the Continent. Mary never saw him again.

The war between France and Spain, into which England was now dragged, had been started by Pope Paul IV, an old man of eighty, whose ruling passion was hatred of the Spaniards and all their works. It was the Spaniards who had subdued Italy, and conquered Paul's native city of Naples. He now excommunicated King Philip and called upon the French to help expel the Spaniards from Italy. So Mary, most devout of the Pope's servants, now found herself joining a league against the Holy Father at the bidding of an excommunicate husband. The war was extremely unpopular in England. Its only result was the loss of Calais – 'a jewel useless and costly, but dearly prized' – the last link with Edward III's victory at Crécy two hundred years earlier.

War with France

The loss of Calais (January 1558) was a bitter blow to the nation's pride – no less bitter to the dying Queen. Men's thoughts, she well knew, were turning to her young sister Elizabeth, in the hope of better times. And Elizabeth, she knew even better, would undo all her work. Nevertheless, under pressure from her ministers, she acknowledged Elizabeth as her successor. Not long afterwards, one dark November morning, messengers rode out from St. James's Palace towards Hatfield, where the 25-year-old Princess was waiting. The messengers hailed the accession of Queen Elizabeth. The reign of Mary was over. Honest but misguided, courageous but unfortunate, above all lacking sufficient time, the first Tudor Queen had failed to achieve her ambitions.

Loss of Calais 1558

Death of Mary 1558

4. Elizabeth and the Church Settlement

Elizabeth, the daughter of Anne Boleyn, was born in 1533, at a time when her father was taking the fateful steps which led to the breach with Rome. During the reigns of her father, brother, and sister she had seen the English Reformation pass through three stages, and

Elizabeth 1558-1603

with each of these in turn she herself had to conform. First, there was Henry VIII's political reform, a Catholic England without the Pope. Secondly, there came, under Edward VI, the Protestant advance influenced by foreign reformers, and marked by the abandonment of the old ritual and by the issue of the Prayer Book in English, as well as by a pillage of the churches. Thirdly, there was the Catholic Revival under Mary and Philip, and the burnings that made the Reformation live. The fourth stage fell to Elizabeth – the settlement of the Church after these three violent changes which had divided the country. In attempting to settle the country, Elizabeth scorned 'the falsehood of extremes'; both her character and her policy favoured compromise – and a Church that tried to find room for all, those still attached to Catholic practices and Protestants. Her great minister, William Cecil, was of the same way of thinking. Cecil had been Protector Somerset's secretary; he had been Protestant under Edward and had gone to Mass under Mary. It was Elizabeth and Cecil, who, with Parliament's aid, arranged the Church Settlement of 1559.

Act of Supremacy 1559

First, the Marian legislation which had reconciled England with the Pope was repealed, and a new Act of Supremacy was passed in 1559 declaring the Sovereign to be 'supreme of all persons and causes, ecclesiastical as well as civil, within this realm'. Elizabeth avoided her father's title of Supreme Head, and instead became Supreme Governor, which was less offensive to Catholics and acknowledged that 'the ministry of God's Word and of the Sacraments' does not belong to the Crown. Nevertheless, the right of the Crown to control the Church was closely guarded. The Royal Supremacy was very real, and Elizabeth resented any attempt by Parliament to advise her on Church policy.

Act of Uniformity 1559

Secondly, the use of the Second Prayer Book of Edward VI, with modifications in favour of the older practices, was made compulsory by the Act of Uniformity of 1559. This Act compelled the clergy to use the Prayer Book, and it also compelled the laity to go to church and hear the English service read. 'All and every person within this realm shall diligently and faithfully ... resort to their parish church ... upon every Sunday and Holy Days, and then and there to abide, orderly and soberly, during the time of the Common Prayer, Readings, and other service of God there to be ministered.' The penalty for non-attendance was a fine of twelve pence (that would be many pounds in our money), 'for the maintenance of the poor'.

By these twin Acts of Supremacy and Uniformity the main lines of Elizabeth's Church Settlement were laid down. The papal supremacy was once again overthrown, and the English service was made uniform and compulsory. To see that her orders in religious matters were carried out, the Queen appointed the Court of High Commission, a kind of Privy Council for the Church, and to some known as 'the Protestant Inquisition'. This Court punished absentees from church, dealt with clerical offences, and administered the oath under the Act of Supremacy to all judges, mayors, and other officials. It met first in 1559, and it deprived of their offices the whole bench of Romanist bishops and about 190 of the clergy.

In many ways the settlement was on moderate lines. The oath, under the new Act of Supremacy, was demanded only from the clergy and from persons in official positions, not from all subjects. Again, certain parts of Edward's Prayer Book, which were specially offensive to Romanists, were omitted (e.g. the insulting clause in the Litany which referred to 'the tyranny of the Bishop of Rome and all his detestable enormities'). The settlement, Elizabeth hoped, would not offend the main body of English men and women and they would gradually get used to it. But, even for those who still clung to the papal supremacy or objected to the English service, there was to be no active persecution. The sword and the stake were not to be the normal engines of the new government. Matthew Parker, Elizabeth's first Archbishop of Canterbury (1559-75), was careful not to make too many Catholics into traitors by tendering the oath to them a second time if they refused it at the first. Unhappily, this moderation did not last throughout the reign, for reasons which will appear presently.

Character of the Elizabethan settlement

The legislation of 1559 may be regarded as a settlement in two ways. First, it laid down the lines on which the Church of England has proceeded ever since; secondly, it brought peace for the time being. There were various religious wars in Europe during the second half of the sixteenth century, but not in England. But, if the settlement of 1559 ended the long period of changes of the previous twenty-five years, in another way it opened a new era of controversy, which lasted over a hundred years. In practice, the settlement was opposed by two sorts of people – the Papists and the Puritans. By the end of Elizabeth's reign there were three religious groups in England – the Anglicans, who supported the Elizabethan settlement; the Papists, who rejected the settlement and hoped for its replacement by Roman Catholicism; and the Puritans, who accepted the settlement for the time being, but hoped to remove what they saw as its imperfections and make it more fully Protestant. Almost everyone agreed that national unity depended on there being one religion uniformly imposed throughout the country and yet agreement was lacking about what this religion should be. Finally, the issue had to be solved by allowing different religious groups to go their own way, but before that happened, after the Revolution of 1688, religious controversy had contributed to civil war.

5. The Scottish Reformation

(i) *The House of Stuart.*

The story of the Reformation in Scotland was closely bound up with the fortunes of England and with the future of Great Britain. Before tracing its course a brief retrospect of Scottish history under the House of Stuart is desirable.

Robert I (Bruce), the victor of Bannockburn (1314), was succeeded by his son, David II, who left no heir. The succession therefore passed to the House of Stuart, through David's sister Margaret, wife of Walter Stuart, whose ancestors had been High Stewards (whence Stuarts) of Scotland. Margaret's son was Robert II, the first of the Stuart kings (1370-90). After Robert II came Robert III, whose eldest son was killed by the nobles; the other son, James, was captured by the English and spent many years in captivity. Then follows the 'mournful procession of the five Jameses'. All these kings, except James V, who died of a broken heart, came to a violent end. All of them except James IV (who succeeded at eighteen) came to the throne as children, and therefore four reigns began with a minority and a regency. This was a great evil in days when a turbulent people needed a strong ruler. The melancholy tale of weak government, anarchy, and murder continued with little interruption throughout the fifteenth century.

The Five Jameses

At the time of his father's death, James I was eleven years old, and a prisoner in England. When, after twenty years' captivity, he returned to his native land, he tried to reduce the country to order. But a party of barons broke into his castle one night and murdered him. James II, succeeding at six, grew up to quarrel with the powerful House of Douglas; he invited the chief of the Douglases to dine with him, and then murdered him in cold blood. James III, succeeding at eight, grew up to suffer the usual fate. He was a cultured man, who had nothing in common with the wild 'lairds' of Scotland. One of them, Archibald Douglas, rebelled against him, and defeated him in battle. From this field James III rode away wounded, and took refuge in a cottage. There, as his enemies gave out, he 'happenit to be slain'.

The reign of James IV (1488-1513) was less disorderly, chiefly because for once there was no royal minority. For a time there seemed to be a prospect both of peace at home and, what was equally unusual, peace with England; for James IV married Margaret, daughter of Henry VII. But later on he quarrelled with his brother-in-law, Henry

VIII, turned away from the English connection, and renewed the old alliance with France. He was slain, with most of his nobles, on the bloody field of Flodden (1513).

His son, James V (1513-42), succeeded at the age of two; there was the usual long minority. When he grew up he drifted into war with his uncle Henry VIII. He sent an army across the border, but it was utterly routed near Carlisle, at the battle of Solway Moss (1542). James died three weeks later, leaving an infant daughter to succeed him – Mary Queen of Scots. After Somerset's victory at Pinkie (1547), as we have seen, Mary was sent to France to marry the Dauphin, afterwards Francis II. In 1561 she returned to Scotland, a widow of nineteen.

Scotland, in the fifteenth and sixteenth centuries, was still a land where lawless lairds took advantage of the weakness of the monarchy to pursue their own private feuds and ambitions. Murder was an everyday occurrence, and the country was a prey to disorder. But beyond the Lowlands was an even more unruly land – the wild north of the Highlanders, who could not be brought under even such government as existed in the Lowlands. It was a country with these traditions which was suddenly confronted with the problems of the Reformation.

(ii) *John Knox.*

The condition of the Church in Scotland, during the later medieval period, was as deplorable as that of the country. The Church possessed a large share of the wealth of a poor land: it was said to own almost half the revenue of the kingdom. The younger sons of nobles, and the illegitimate sons of kings, were greedy for Church lands, which they obtained in the most shameless way. A son of James IV was already Archbishop of St. Andrews when he was killed at Flodden at the age of twenty. James V persuaded Pope Clement VII to bestow the abbeys of Kelso, Melrose, and Holyrood upon three of his illegitimate sons. This shameless traffic in Church property was

Death of
James 1542

The Church
of Scotland

one of the reasons why the Scottish Reformation, when it came, was so violent.

The scandalous life of the Scottish clergy was, no doubt, connected with unsuitable appointments to high positions in the Church. A Council at Edinburgh (1549) complained of 'the corruption of morals and profane lewdness of life in churchmen of almost all ranks, together with crass ignorance of literature and of all the liberal arts'.[18] Men who could hardly read or write were admitted to the priesthood, which they then disgraced by the evil manner of their lives. It is a black picture. In the reign of James V, with the introduction of Tyndale's New Testament (c. 1525), the new reforming doctrines began to spread. One of the most prominent Protestant martyrs was Patrick Hamilton, a great-grandson of James II, who was burnt at St. Andrews (1528). Nearly twenty years later George Wishart, a prominent preacher, was also burnt at the stake. His friends in revenge burst into the castle of St. Andrews and murdered Cardinal Beaton, the head of the Scottish Church (1546). The Scottish tradition of the blood feud was thus applied to religious disputes.

Reformers in Scotland

After the murder of Beaton his assassins defended the castle; but after two months they surrendered to a French fleet, which had been sent to help the government. Among the prisoners was a Protestant named John Knox, who now spent a year and a half as a slave on a French galley. After his release, Knox went to England, where he became a chaplain of Edward VI. Then, on the accession of Mary Tudor, he made a journey through France and Switzerland. At Geneva he met and became the disciple of Calvin, the famous Protestant reformer. He paid a short visit to Scotland in 1555; four years later he came back for good, to become the leader of the Scottish Reformation.

John Knox

John Calvin was a Frenchman who, after the death of Luther (1546), became the leading Protestant thinker. He was based in

Calvin

---

[18] Rait, *History of Scotland*.

Geneva and ruled that city with a rod of iron for twenty years till his death (1564). Calvin set out to create not only a new Church but a new society, in which men should be compelled to live and act like Christians. To him, the final authority in the State was not the prince (as with Luther) but the community – the 'congregation', ruled by elders or 'presbyters' and ministers, not by bishops and priests, for whom Calvin had no use. His followers in Scotland and England (and later in America) were known as Presbyterians; in France as Huguenots; and parts of Germany and the Netherlands preferred his creed to Luther's. Under his rule Geneva dealt sternly with sinners or heretics. To Knox it was 'the most perfect school of Christ that ever was on earth since the days of the Apostles'; to the Pope it was 'a nest of devils'; to many others it seemed, with its stern ideals, the home of a harsh, gloomy, and tyrannical system.

Mary Queen of Scots and France

The progress of the Reformation in Scotland was bound up with politics. The influence of France was much resented by a section of the nobles. Not only was the Queen living in France, married to the Dauphin (1558), but her French mother, Mary of Guise, was regent of Scotland. 'Scotland a province of France!' was the cry of these lords, who banded themselves together in an association called the Lords of the Congregation. They allied themselves with the Protestant reformers, and so obtained the powerful aid of John Knox, who disliked the French almost as much as he disliked the Pope. He wrote a pamphlet called *The First Blast of the Trumpet against the Monstrous Regiment of Women*, which was an attack on the regiment (or rule) of the three Queens, Mary of England, Mary of Scotland, and Mary of Guise. The first of these Marys soon afterwards died; her successor, Elizabeth, was so offended at the aspersions cast on her sex by Knox that she refused him a passage through England.

Knox returns 1559

But, in the eventful year 1559, Knox landed at Leith. That summer he preached his famous sermon at Perth – 'Burn the nests, and the rooks will fly' – which let loose the fury of the mob on the property of the Church. The result was an orgy of destruction in the Scottish monasteries (1560), like that which had already taken place in England. There was riot and destruction in Perth following Knox's sermon. A month later the Calvinist mob laid in ruins the noble Cathedral of St. Andrews, and all its priceless treasures were destroyed or carried away. Knox tried and failed to prevent the sack of the Abbey and Palace of Scone; he was no longer able to control the fury which he had unchained.

Mary Stuart was now Queen of France. Her husband, Francis II (1559-60), sent an army to hold the fortress of Leith, while Mary of Guise took refuge from the Lords of the Congregation in Edinburgh Castle. Now or never was the time for Elizabeth to intervene; the Scots lords had already begged her to do so. For once she cast aside her hesitations, and sent an English force to the north. English and Scots laid siege to Leith, and though the assault failed, the French garrison had to give way under pressure of famine. Just then the regent died. The French signed the Treaty of Edinburgh (1560), by which they undertook to leave Scotland, which, since the English also departed, was left in the hands of John Knox and the Lords of the Congregation. It was a signal triumph for the forces of the Reformation. To England the Treaty of Edinburgh was of great importance, for it ensured a Protestant Scotland, and, what was equally remarkable, a grateful Scotland. Had affairs gone differently – had the French taken Edinburgh, had Mary of Guise lived to triumph over the Reformers, not only Scottish but English history might have been completely altered.

Treaty of Edinburgh 1560

For Scotland the events of the year 1559-60 formed the turning point in her history. The victorious reformers summoned a Parliament (1560), at which the papal authority was rejected, the monasteries dissolved, and the celebration of the Mass made illegal. Knox and his friends drew up a 'Confession of Faith', which established the Scottish Kirk, described by them as 'One company and multitude of men chosen by God, who rightly worship and embrace Him by true faith in Christ Jesus'. The Kirk was ruled by

The Scottish Kirk

elders or presbyters and ministers, like Calvin's Congregation. Under Knox's successor, Andrew Melville, the office of bishop was declared unnecessary and illegal.

Thus the old religion was overthrown in Scotland, and the scarcely less ancient feud with England subsided. Elizabeth, much though she disliked religious excesses, was the friend of the new Scotland – but not of Scotland's Queen, though at first she greeted her with fair words. Mary Stuart stood for all that her Calvinist subjects hated, which may be summed up in the two words, France and Rome. That year (1560) she ceased to be Queen of France, for her husband Francis II died suddenly in December. Next summer Mary took ship for her northern kingdom. She left behind the capital where she had reigned as Europe's most beautiful Queen; she left the people, the customs, the religion she loved. She sailed north through the mists, to what was to be her home. But there was only the cold bleakness of Holyrood to welcome her – that and the harsh cries of outlandish men, some of whom hammered on the door of her private chapel, during the celebration of Mass, with cries of 'Death to the priest!' The stage was set for the tragedy of Mary Stuart. 'Over her devoted head were to break the thunders of a ruining world; her weapons were but a fair face, and a subtle tongue, and an indomitable courage.'[19]

Mary returns
1561

---

[19] Andrew Lang, *History of Scotland*.

Date Summary: Early Tudor Period
(1485-1558)

BRITISH ISLES	AFRICA, ASIA, AMERICA	EUROPE

HENRY VII (1485-1509)

1485 ⚔ Bosworth		
	1487 Diaz at the Cape	
	1492 Columbus	
1494 Poynings' Law		
1498 Colet met Erasmus	1498 Vasco da Gama (India)	
	1500 Cabral (Brazil)	
1502 James IV (Scotland) married		

HENRY VIII (1509-47)

1513 ⚔ Flodden. James IV *d.*		
1515 Wolsey Chancellor		1515-47 Francis I (France)
1516 More's *Utopia*		
		1517 LUTHER'S THESES
	1519 Cortez in Mexico	1519-56 Emp. Charles V
		1519 Leonardo da Vinci *d.*
1521 Henry VII *Fidei Defensor*	1521 Magellan killed	1521 Diet of Worms
		1525 ⚔ Pavia
1527 DIVORCE QUESTION		1527 Sack of Rome
1529-36 The Reformation Parliament		
1530 Wolsey *d.*		
	1532 Pizarro (Peru)	
1534 Act of Supremacy	1534 Cartier (Canada)	
1535 More and Fisher executed		
1536-40 Dissolution of the Monasteries		
1537 The Great Bible		
		1540 Loyola (Society of Jesus)
		1541 Calvin at Geneva
1542 James V (Scotland) *d.*		
		1543 Copernicus *d.*

EDWARD VI (1547-53)

1549 First Prayer Book		
Act of Uniformity		
1552 Somerset executed		

MARY I (1553-58)

1554 Philip and Mary married		
		1555 Peace of Augsburg
1556 Cranmer executed		1556 Emp. Charles V abdicated

V

THE POLICY OF ELIZABETH

1. Elizabeth: England and Europe

Queen
Elizabeth
1558-1603

ENGLAND under Queen Elizabeth is an inspiring theme. The two great achievements which we associate with this reign – the maintenance of English independence against Spain, and the work of the poets and dramatists – are matters of which every Englishman can be proud; for it is no small thing to have beaten off the attack of a great world power, and to have produced one of the world's greatest literatures. The success of the reign was due to the work of an able, scheming woman, helped by chosen ministers. Elizabeth won her way through a difficult and perilous situation, not by bold, straightforward methods, not by a display of force, but by a cunning and frequently underhand policy. Her task was nothing less than to save and establish the religious and political independence of England.

Cecil and
Walsingham

Elizabeth's chief minister for forty years was William Cecil. He was principal Secretary till 1572, when he was made Treasurer, and given the title of Lord Burghley. His successor as Secretary was Sir Francis Walsingham. Cecil stood for a cautious policy, and he was averse from any activity which might provoke war with Spain. Walsingham, on the other hand, was a more ardent Protestant, and he was in favour of stern measures against English Catholics, even if such action should lead to a Spanish war; he was in fact the chief agent in tracking down the numerous plots against Elizabeth's life.

With all her faults, Elizabeth was a consummate politician in an age when politics was supposed to be a man's game and women were supposed to be subordinate to men. She avoided becoming the puppet of any one councillor by maintaining a balance of opinions and groups on her Council. She presented herself as a special woman,

ELIZABETH I (1533-1603, REIGN: 1558-1603)
(Portrait, c. 1600, by Isaac Oliver.)

virgin mother of her people, and favoured by God. Indeed, she had need of divine favour, for she had many enemies. In the eyes of the Pope and of Catholic Europe her parents had never been married and therefore she was illegitimate.[20] Her reign cannot be understood without some appreciation of the perils which confronted England during the first thirty years of her reign.

The perils of the reign

During that period there were three grave dangers, any one of which might have overwhelmed England had Elizabeth died before her task was complete. First, since orthodox Catholics regarded Mary Stuart as the rightful Queen of England, there was the danger of civil war following a disputed succession; second, there was the danger of a religious war between Protestants and Catholics; third, there was the danger of foreign invasion and conquest. In practice, the third of these dangers eventually counteracted the other two; for in the face of threatened foreign invasion (in the year of the Armada) all other quarrels were laid aside. But for the thirty years before the Armada, the outbreak of civil war combined with religious strife was a constant menace. The Queen's life alone stood between England and anarchy. If she had died – or had been assassinated – many of her subjects would have disputed the succession of Mary of Scotland, and the horrors of civil war might have returned. Not only this: Mary Stuart was a Catholic, and her succession might have been followed by an attempt to restore Romanism, which in its turn might have led to a 'religious' war. Englishmen had only to look across the Channel to Holland or to France to see what that would have meant. For in both those countries a hideous strife between Protestants and Catholics was being carried on during the greater part of Elizabeth's reign.

Elizabeth could not imitate her father, Henry VIII, by boldly destroying every obstacle which stood in her path. She was unsuited

---

[20] Her mother's marriage had, in any case, been annulled. Both she and Mary succeeded to the throne under the will of Henry VIII, who had been empowered by Parliament to arrange the succession.

by temperament to do so, and the obstacles were too serious. The situation in Europe had changed considerably since the days of her father. In Henry's day Catholic Europe, demoralized and unprepared, was still staggering under the first onslaught of the Reformation. Since then there had been a civil war in Germany, followed by the religious Peace of Augsburg (1555). Germany thereafter remained more or less quiet; and her Protestant princes, secure in their own lands, did not become powerful outside the Empire. Catholic Spain, on the other hand, was enormously powerful; Philip II (1556–98) was at the head of one of the greatest empires the world had ever seen. Unlike his father, Charles V, he had no German Reformation to distract his attention. If he had been able to combine his power with that of the second greatest Catholic king in Europe – the King of France – there would have been little hope for the survival of English Protestantism, or indeed of English independence. *The Spanish power*

A Catholic crusade against England seemed at one time quite possible. For the Catholic position had greatly improved, owing to the reforms within the Catholic Church, which are usually called the Counter-Reformation. The Popes of this period were very different from the easy-going Popes of the Renaissance. Men like Pius V or Sixtus V were more concerned with the revival of the Church than with art or literature or their power in Italy. They came to emphasise again papal spiritual leadership. This change in the character of the Papacy was accompanied by drastic reforms in the discipline of the Church. At the various sittings of the Council of Trent (1545-63), Catholic doctrine was more clearly defined, and the need for reform recognized. At the same time the Courts of the Inquisition waged war on heretics in Italy and stamped out the remains of heresy in Spain. Besides all this, the success of the Jesuits accounted for much. The Society of Jesus was founded in 1540 by Ignatius Loyola, an ardent and pious young Spanish nobleman. His followers became the vanguard of the Catholic crusade against heretics and infidels the *The Counter-Reformation* *The Jesuits* world over. Their elaborate system of education enabled them to train the young to a life especially devoted to the papal service. There had been no such enthusiastic teachers and preachers as the Jesuits since the days of St. Dominic. So, with a reformed Papacy, a redisciplined Church, and an active crusade led by the Jesuits, it seemed that the great days of the Church of Rome were returning.

The chances that the Catholic powers would combine to dethrone Elizabeth and destroy English Protestantism were undermined by the rivalry of France and Spain. Yet if these Powers would not combine, they might act separately. Philip, however, would not permit the French to place Mary Queen of Scots on the English throne, for then both England and Scotland would become mere provinces of France. But Philip might take action himself. This is what Elizabeth tried to prevent; and for thirty years she succeeded.

It was Elizabeth's design to avoid open war with Philip. At the same time she lost no opportunity of injuring him, and there were several ways in which this could be done. For example, she gave secret encouragement to her sailors to set out on piratical expeditions to the Spanish Main,[21] while protesting to the Spanish ambassador that she knew nothing about such matters. Again, she interested herself in the weak spot of Philip's empire – the Netherlands. The inhabitants of these rich Low Countries, one of the chief markets of Europe, disliked the control of the Court of Madrid, and they began a struggle for their independence. For more than forty years Philip and his successor strove to quell the rebellious spirit of these Dutchmen, but without success. In 1567 Philip sent the ruthless Duke of Alva to govern the Netherlands; Alva ruled by means of a council well named the Council of Blood. But the desire for independence in the Netherlands had become mixed up with the advance of Protestantism, and these motives combined were too strong even for

Elizabeth and Spain

The Netherlands

---

[21] 'Spanish Main', that is, the mainland of America adjacent to the Caribbean Sea.

Alva. Calvinism took a great hold of the northern provinces (the modern Holland), which formed the backbone of the resistance to Philip. The leadership of the great nobleman William of Orange was one great asset to the rebels; the plucky fighting of the Sea-Beggars – as the Dutch sailors were called – was another. The Sea-Beggars used English harbours as bases from which to raid the Spanish shipping which passed through the Straits of Dover. Elizabeth connived at this; she also, from time to time, sent the rebels money, although she hated to part with it.

A similar policy dictated Elizabeth's attitude to the Wars of Religion in France. Here again the Calvinists, called Huguenots, were causing trouble. The reigns of Charles IX and Henry III were one long record of civil war and bloodshed. Elizabeth occasionally helped the Huguenots, though half-heartedly; here again she played a double game, for she was careful to avoid an open breach with the French king.

France

One other factor further complicated the situation – the prospect of the Queen's marriage. Elizabeth refused Philip's offer of marriage (1559); she dallied, however, with various other suitors, including two brothers of Charles IX of France. But none of these marriage negotiations, though long continued, came to anything. She recalled how Englishmen had reacted when her sister's marriage brought the prospect of a foreign King. At the beginning of her reign Elizabeth became infatuated with Robert Dudley (son of Northumberland), whom she afterwards made Earl of Leicester. Cecil feared that she would marry Dudley, and perhaps she considered doing so. There was a scandal in 1560, when Dudley's wife Amy Robsart was found dead in suspicious circumstances. Dudley was under a cloud for a time, but he held his position as first man in the kingdom – which he certainly did not deserve – till his death in 1588. Elizabeth gave up the idea of marrying him – if she ever really entertained it – and even suggested Leicester as a husband for Mary Queen of Scots. Parliament frequently petitioned the Queen to marry, and ensure the

The Queen's marriage question

succession. She told the members (1563) that 'if any think I never meant to try that life, they be deceived'. But she never married, realising perhaps that if she married a subject, she would attract the hostility of all his enemies. What is more, she was long able to remain on tolerably good terms with the rivals, France and Spain, who were both anxious to win her support. If by marriage she had definitely thrown in her lot with one of them, she would have been at once faced with the open hostility of the other, and this was what she strove to prevent. Gambling that the succession problem could eventually be solved without her marrying and producing a child seemed the better option.

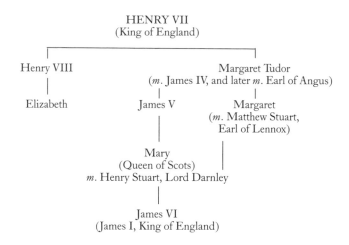

2. The Fall of Mary Queen of Scots

For the first nine years of Elizabeth's reign Mary Stuart reigned as Queen of Scotland; and then for nineteen years she was Elizabeth's prisoner. The events leading to Mary's fall were of great importance in the course of English history.

MARY STUART OR MARY, QUEEN OF SCOTS (1542-1587)

When she had been in Scotland four years, Mary married (1565). Mary
Her choice fell on her cousin, Lord Darnley, who was a grandson of marries
Margaret Tudor by her second husband. The joint claims to the Darnley 1565
English throne of Mary and Darnley, as descendants of Henry VII,
were very strong. For, since Catholic Europe considered Elizabeth
illegitimate, Mary was, in Catholic eyes, the rightful Queen of

111

England. Now she had married a man who could also claim descent from an English King, and, like Mary, Darnley was a Catholic.

But, unlike her cousin Elizabeth, Mary was a woman who allowed passions, both of love and hatred, to master her; and this brought about her ruin. She soon tired of her weak, worthless husband. For his part, Darnley was jealous of the Queen, and at last did her an unpardonable injury. He and his friends broke into Mary's private room at Holyrood, where she was supping with her Italian secretary, David Rizzio. The intruders drew their swords, and Rizzio sheltered behind the Queen. But they dragged him from her, and murdered him in the doorway – almost in her sight. She could never forgive Darnley for this outrage. But, with great cunning, she pretended to be reconciled to him, and even persuaded the foolish man to help her escape from Edinburgh – out of the way of his fellow murderers. Soon after this her son, the future James VI, was born. The next year Darnley fell ill. Mary, still pretending to be friendly, brought him to a house called Kirk-o'-Field, outside Edinburgh. That night Kirk-o'-Field was blown up by gunpowder, and Darnley's body was found in the garden outside (1567). There is little doubt that the murderer was the Earl of Bothwell. But did he act with Mary's knowledge and consent? The view to be taken of that disputed question depends on the genuineness of the 'Casket Letters' – found in a silver gilt casket which one of Bothwell's men delivered up in order to escape torture. 'If the letters are what they seem to be, the letters of the Queen to Bothwell, then Mary is implicated in the murder of her husband. If they are not authentic, there is no evidence of her guilt.'[22] The problem remains unsolved to this day.

Murder of Darnley 1567

Fall of Mary 1567

Two months after the murder, Bothwell carried off Mary to Dunbar, divorced his wife, and re-entered Edinburgh with the Queen by his side, which convinced many people that Mary had

---

[22] Acton, *Lectures on Modern History*, pp. 149-52

indeed been complicit in her dead husband's murder. Mary's love for Bothwell was her ruin. She married him (1567), but even then she was unhappy, knowing that Bothwell, though a fascinating cavalier, was a worthless character. The Scottish lords, led by her half-brother, the Earl of Moray, rose against Bothwell, and defeated the Queen and her husband at the battle of Carberry Hill. Bothwell escaped, but Mary was captured and imprisoned in Loch Leven Castle. She was forced to sign her abdication (1567), and her infant son was crowned King of Scotland as James VI. Next year Mary escaped from Loch Leven, and made one more attempt to regain her throne. The Hamiltons and some other friends joined her, but again her friends were defeated (battle of Langside, 1568). This time the Queen escaped from the field and fled to England. She wrote to Elizabeth asking for her help. Elizabeth sent an escort, and Mary was brought from Carlisle to Bolton Castle in Yorkshire. There she remained for the time being – out of the reach of rescue.

Elizabeth's prisoner

3. The Catholic Plots (1568-87)

The situation, as far as Elizabeth was concerned, had now considerably improved. Scotland settled down to its usual royal minority, and James VI was brought up a Protestant. If the French tried to set Mary on the English throne, they would no longer find friends in Scotland to assist them. There remained, however, the danger that the English Catholics would prefer Mary to Elizabeth and attempt to make her Queen. The first such attempt – the Rising in the North – was made shortly after Mary landed in England.

The north of England was much more Catholic than the south, and it was from the north that the trouble came. The Earls of Northumberland and Westmorland agreed to raise troops and free Mary; the Duke of Norfolk was involved in a plot to marry her. Mary sent a message to King Philip that if he would send help, she

The Northern Rising 1569

would be Queen of England in three months, and the Mass would be said all over the country. Fortunately for Elizabeth, Philip was almost as cautious and hesitating a person as she was herself. The Pope urged him to action, but even the fact that Elizabeth at that moment seized some Spanish treasure-ships on their way to Holland did not move him to an open breach with England. All he would do was to 'encourage with money and secret favour the Catholics of the North'. Philip in fact preferred playing at the half-measures at which Elizabeth herself was such an expert. While he was hesitating, the Catholics of the north rebelled (1569). The Earls of Northumberland and Westmorland took Durham; they entered the cathedral and heard Mass, then publicly burnt the English Prayer Book and the English Bible. They marched as far as Tadcaster in Yorkshire, but here they lost heart and began to retreat. Their forces melted away, and the leaders escaped to Scotland. But Elizabeth, like her father after the Pilgrimage of Grace, took a cruel revenge on the north. Gallows were erected on every village green, and between six and seven hundred rebels were hanged. The Queen gave particular instructions that an example was to be made in every village; if only one man from a village had joined the rebellion, that man was to be hanged.

Pius V excomm- unicates Elizabeth 1570

The next move came from the Pope, Pius V, who issued a Bull of Excommunication against Elizabeth (1570). In it he declared that English Catholics were released from their allegiance to the heretic queen. The situation was dangerous; the more so as Mary was still intriguing with Spain. Her agent was a Florentine banker named Ridolfi, her chief English supporter the Duke of Norfolk. Ridolfi went to Rome for the papal blessing on the plot. Then he went to

Ridolfi Plot 1571

Spain, and proposed to the Spanish Council that, as a first step, Elizabeth should be assassinated; as a second, that Alva should invade England from the Netherlands. But while Philip was slowly debating, Cecil had discovered the whole plot. The alarm caused by the northern rebellion, the excommunication of the Queen, and the

Ridolfi Plot, was reflected in Elizabeth's Parliament of 1571, which passed an Act making it high treason for an English subject to introduce a Papal Bull into England – in retaliation for the Pope's action in the previous year. Next, the Spanish ambassador was expelled; and the Duke of Norfolk was tried for high treason and condemned to death. Elizabeth hesitated for some time before signing his death warrant, but finally did so, while refusing Parliament's demand for the execution of Mary (1572).

Execution of Norfolk 1572

Cecil was so alarmed at the intrigues of the English Catholics with the Spaniards that he arranged an alliance with France (Treaty of Blois, April 1572), by which England practically committed herself to join France in assisting the Netherlands against Spain. This alliance was continued even after the shock of the Massacre of St. Bartholomew, four months later (August 1572), when thousands of Huguenots were brutally murdered in the streets of Paris by the orders of Catherine de Medici, the French King's mother.

French alliance

Massacre of St. Bartholomew 1572

The next Catholic challenge to Elizabeth arose in Ireland, where the English policy of colonising the country and uprooting its Gaelic culture brought about an alliance of the Irish with Counter Reformation Catholicism and created strong anti-English feeling. The result was the rebellion of the Earl of Desmond (1579), and to assist it the Pope openly sent a body of Italian soldiers, and Philip II secretly provided some Spaniards. But the Irish rebellion was crushed and Desmond slain.

The Jesuits in Ireland

Meanwhile, an active Catholic mission began its work in England. A former Oxford teacher, William Allen, set up a college for catholic Englishmen at Douai in the Netherlands. By the late 1570s, Douai priests, soon joined by Jesuits, were busy in England. The most famous Jesuits, Parsons (formerly Fellow of Balliol) and Campion, landed in 1580. Parliament, seriously alarmed, passed a severe Act, which made the attempt to convert the Queen's subjects to Roman Catholicism a treasonable offence, and forbade the hearing of the Mass under a huge financial penalty and a year's imprisonment. The fine

The Jesuits in England

for Catholic recusants (i.e. those who refused to attend an Anglican church) was raised to £20 a month. Shortly afterwards Campion was seized in Berkshire, tried for conspiring with the Queen's enemies, tortured to make him reveal his confederates, and executed with the usual barbarity (1581). Two years later (1583) a Catholic gentleman of Cheshire, named Throckmorton, plotted for a Spanish invasion in favour of Mary, and in this plot Father Parsons was involved.

Execution of Campion 1581

The first Jesuit martyr, Edmund Campion, was a good and sincere man; his execution was a pitiable tragedy. His enthusiasm for his religion had made him a papal agent; yet he was probably not a willing supporter of the papal policy of undermining the loyalty of Elizabeth's subjects. But the Pope could scarcely be surprised if, after he had actually sent troops to a part of the Queen's dominions – Ireland – Elizabeth took steps to crush Catholic missionaries in England. The persecution of Catholics went on for the rest of Elizabeth's reign. The torture of Catholic prisoners in the Tower, by the rack and other means, was considered necessary in order to make prisoners reveal the names of their accomplices. The Government justified its cruelty by the danger of the situation, and by the fact that it was now in theory impossible to remain at the same time a loyal Catholic and a loyal subject of Elizabeth. The Catholic subjects of the Queen thus found themselves in a distressing dilemma. Persecuted for adherence to their faith, impoverished by ruinous fines, they were at any moment liable to be seized, tortured, and put to death for the crime of treason – a crime which most of them had no desire to commit. But when Catholics were executed, it was for treason, not for their religion.

Persecution of Catholics

In 1584 an event occurred abroad which increased the alarm of Cecil and Walsingham. William of Orange, the heroic leader of the revolted Dutch subjects of Philip II, was assassinated by order of the Spanish King. The thought was in every Englishman's mind that it would be Elizabeth's turn next. A National Association was formed by various Protestant gentlemen 'to withstand and revenge to the

Assassination of William of Orange 1584

uttermost all such malicious actions and attempts against Her Majesty's most royal person'. Parliament legalized this Association next year (1585). By another Act all Jesuits were banished from the realm on pain of death, and the harbouring of a Jesuit was made a felony.

The hopes of the captive Queen Mary and of her supporters were still centred on Philip of Spain. Philip was still undecided whether to support Mary more actively. Neither Elizabeth nor Philip ever actually declared war; they drifted into it. War came considerably nearer in 1585. In that year Drake conducted a destructive raid on the West Indies; this was his reply to Philip's action in laying an embargo on English ships in Spanish ports. At the same time the plight of the Dutch rebels since the murder of William of Orange convinced Walsingham, and finally the Queen herself, that something must be done to help them. A treaty was accordingly signed with the rebels (1585), and in the same year the Earl of Leicester landed in Holland with 6,000 men. The following year, without consulting Elizabeth, Leicester had himself proclaimed Governor General of the Netherlands; the Queen was angry, but allowed him to retain the title. The new Governor, however, soon found himself in difficulties; he became involved in the endless quarrels between the various parties in the Netherlands. He issued a decree prohibiting commerce with the enemy on pain of death. Had this edict been enforced it would have crippled the Spanish armies; but it could not be enforced because it would have crippled the Netherlanders as well. The prosperity of the Netherlands seaports depended on overseas trade; they argued, not without reason, that if their trade were ruined there would be no money to continue the war. The surrender of Zutphen by two treacherous Englishmen (Catholics formerly in the Spanish service) added to the unpopularity of Leicester and his men;[23] the

Leicester in the Netherlands 1585-7

---

[23] The chivalrous conduct of Sir Philip Sidney – courtier, scholar, soldier – who was mortally wounded in this campaign, sheds one ray of interest on this rather dull and sordid affair.

last straw was the failure to relieve Sluys (1587). The same year Leicester, broken in health, threw up his command, and returned to England to die. The expedition cost Elizabeth eighteen months' revenue, and Leicester most of his private fortune.

The
Babington
Plot 1586

In England the plots and counterplots of the past thirty years came to a head in the Babington Conspiracy (1586), in which the most desperate of Mary's adherents in England hatched a plot to murder Elizabeth and to place Mary on the throne with Spanish help. The conspirators were mainly young Catholic gentry, with Anthony Babington at their head, and Father Ballard, a Jesuit on tour in England, as the prime mover. Babington corresponded with Mary, but Walsingham's spies had won over a man called Gifford, one of Mary's servants whom she thought she could trust. Walsingham intercepted the letters, copied them, and then passed them on to their destination. At last there was a letter which showed that Mary was cognizant of the murderous scheme. Then, with all the details of the plot in his hands, Walsingham struck. He placed the evidence before the Queen and then arrested Babington and the other conspirators.

Trial of
Mary 1586

Thirteen of the plotters were executed. Then Mary was tried before a special court at Fotheringhay Castle. She denied the right of the court to try her, an independent sovereign, and protested her entire innocence. She was tried under an Act of 1585 (the same Act which had legalized the Protestant Association) and found guilty of treason. Parliament – on the ground that 'the Queen's safety could in no way be secured as long as the Queen of Scots lived' – then petitioned Elizabeth for Mary's execution. Elizabeth hesitated, and sent a message to Parliament asking whether some other means could be devised for the safety of the kingdom, for she 'could be well pleased to forbear the taking of her blood'. The members replied by repeating their former request. Elizabeth then sent them one of her most characteristic messages: 'If I should say unto you that I mean not to grant your petition, by my faith I should say unto you more than perhaps I mean. And if I should say unto you I mean to grant your petition, I should then tell you more than is fit for you to know. And thus I must deliver you an answer answerless.'

For two months longer Elizabeth hesitated; then she signed the warrant for Mary's execution. Even then she gave no direct orders for the execution to be carried out; but her secretary, Davison, carried the warrant to the Privy Council, who acted without further delay. Mary was accordingly – after nearly twenty years' imprisonment in England – beheaded at Fotheringhay (February 1587), protesting that she died a martyr to the Catholic faith. Her execution 1587

Elizabeth's behaviour when she heard of Mary's execution shows her at her worst. Glossing over the awkward fact that she had signed the death-warrant, she declared that she had never intended the sentence to be carried out. The unfortunate Davison was thrown into prison, tried for acting contrary to the Queen's orders, and ordered to pay an enormous fine. The fine was remitted, but he was kept in prison for three years. In this way Elizabeth attempted to avoid the responsibility for Mary's death by sacrificing her secretary.

4. Traders and Seamen

(i) *Trade with the East.*

The Portuguese discovery of the Cape Route to India, and the foundation of the Spanish Empire in America, had established two great trading monopolies in the world – the Portuguese and the Spanish.[24] This insolent claim, as many Englishmen regarded it, to the monopoly of all the riches of the newly discovered world was bitterly resented by English traders and sailors. The resentment considerably increased with the Reformation, for then to commercial rivalry was added religious intolerance. The Spaniards, who forbade The Spanish and Portuguese Monopolies

---

[24] United after 1580, when Philip II conquered Portugal.

English sailors to trade in their dominions, sometimes treated their enemies badly when they caught them, for to them the English were both heretics and pirates. Tales of Englishmen tortured by the agents of the Inquisition did much to inflame national hatred of the Spaniards during Elizabeth's reign, and indeed for long afterwards.

There were two courses open to English traders; they might try to reach the riches of Asia by a route not in foreign hands, or they might boldly attack the enemy on their own ground. The former course commended itself to Cecil, a peace-loving minister who disliked some of the ventures of men like Francis Drake and John Hawkins, who desired to challenge the Spaniards directly. Cecil classified maritime activity under three heads – trading, fishing, and piracy – 'whereof (he said) the third is detestable and cannot last'. He was mistaken in thinking that piracy could not last – for he underrated Drake's genius – but not in his prophecy that it would lead England into war with Spain. However, the more peaceful kinds of foreign trade, which Cecil encouraged, formed no inconsiderable part of Elizabethan activities. English overseas trade expanded into Europe: the Baltic, German, Mediterranean, and Levant markets were opened up by the Merchant Adventurers, and by the Eastland, Barbary, Venice, and Levant companies.

Cecil's views

Turkey Co. 1581

In 1578 some London merchants sought to revive English trade in the Levant, and sent William Harborne to Constantinople to obtain trading privileges with the Sultan of Turkey. The sultan granted permission, and a Turkey Company was set up (1581), which carried on a lucrative trade. Even here the Spaniards tried to stop the passage of English ships through the Straits of Gibraltar. The Turkey Company afterwards joined forces (1592) with another Mediterranean concern, the Venice Company; after the amalgamation the joint business was known as the Levant Company, and it carried on a successful trade for over two centuries.

Levant Co. 1592

The North-East Passage

A revived interest in the passage to the East via the Arctic regions took place in Mary's reign. Sebastian Cabot, who had sailed to the north-west in his youth, suggested that a new effort should be made towards the north-east. The result was the voyage of Sir Hugh Willoughby and Richard Chancellor to the north of Russia (1553). Willoughby and his crew, who got as far east as Nova Zembla, all perished in the rigours of the Russian winter. Chancellor, more fortunate, reached the port of Archangel, and was conducted to Moscow. It was through this voyage that trade between England and Russia was opened up. A Muscovy Company was established (1553-5) for this purpose and continued to flourish for many years. It sent to Russia an explorer named Anthony Jenkinson, who journeyed down the Volga and crossed the Caspian Sea. Then he pushed eastwards and reached the ancient city of Bokhara, once well known to medieval traders, but here he learnt that the disturbed condition of Central Asia would prevent his reaching China or India by the overland route. He therefore returned to Moscow (1559). Three years later he went again to the East, and reached Persia. An Anglo-Persian trade was then opened up and was continued for nearly twenty years, after which it was abandoned (1579) owing to the inroads of the Turks into Persia. Such were the somewhat unexpected results of the English voyages to Russia.

Willoughby and Chancellor 1553

Jenkinson

The search for the North-West Passage was pursued more vigorously. The voyage of Martin Frobisher (1576) caused great excitement in England, for he not only thought he had discovered the mouth of the Passage (in reality Frobisher Sound) but brought back ore which was said to contain gold. A company called the Cathay Company – the name betrays the false hopes of the promoters – was at once formed. But two more voyages (1577-8) served to show that there was no Passage and no gold. Ten years after this, Captain John Davis continued the search for the Passage, and explored the icy waters between Baffin Land and Greenland (1585-7). All these

Frobisher 1576

voyages, though disappointing in their immediate result, helped to encourage English seamanship.

But neither the North-East nor the North-West Passage was

The East Indies destined to yield fruitful results to their explorers. The true route to the East – via the Cape of Good Hope – was also attempted in Elizabeth's reign. But here there was a danger that the Spaniards might object; and when (in 1582) Edward Fenton, one of Frobisher's captains, set sail for the East Indies, he was instructed not to plunder the property of the Queen's 'friends and allies'. But the Spaniards nevertheless attacked Fenton, and he abandoned the voyage.

A decade later conditions were different; England was at war with Spain, and eager to seize some of the coveted East Indian trade – now, since the absorption of Portugal (1580), in Spanish hands. Two English captains, George Raymond and James Lancaster, sailed for the East in 1591. Raymond's ship sank in a storm with all hands, but

Lancaster's voyages 1591-1601 Lancaster reached the East Indies, where he took two Portuguese ships, and also visited Ceylon. This expedition involved great hardships, and eventually the surviving sailors mutinied and carried off the ship; Lancaster reached home on board a French privateer in 1594. Nevertheless, the eastern project was not abandoned. A

The East India Co. 1600 company – the famous East India Company – was formed in 1600, and Lancaster sailed again for the East in the following year. This time he made a great success of his venture, and returned home with a store of pepper and spices from Java. The East India Company had started on its astonishing career.

(ii) *Colonization.*

Sir Humphrey Gilbert, a Devonshire gentleman, and half-brother

Sir Humphrey Gilbert of Sir Walter Ralegh, was one of the first to interest himself in the North-West Passage. But the failure of Frobisher's expeditions turned Gilbert's thoughts in a new direction. He was among the first to perceive that North America might be a useful discovery in itself, quite apart from the possible existence of a North-West Passage to

India. 'We might inhabit some part of those countries,' he wrote, 'and settle there such needy people of our country, which now trouble the commonwealth, and through want here at home are enforced to commit outrageous offences, whereby they are daily consumed with the gallows.' Gilbert in Newfound-land 1583

Gilbert obtained a patent (1578) from the Queen to 'inhabit and fortify any barbarous lands' not actually in possession of a Christian prince. The same autumn he left England with a fleet of eleven ships, but the following spring they returned, without having accomplished anything. Three years later he set out again with five ships. This time he landed on the island of Newfoundland, and took formal possession of it in the name of the Queen (1583). On the way home Gilbert's ship, the *Squirrel*, was lost with all hands. The account of Gilbert's end was given by a sailor on board the *Golden Hind*, which accompanied the *Squirrel*.

'Gilbert cried out to us, so oft as we did approach within hearing, "We are as near to heaven by sea as by land", reiterating the same speech, well beseeming a soldier, resolute in Jesus Christ, as I can testify he was. The same Monday night, about twelve of the clock, the frigate being ahead of us, suddenly her lights were out, whereof as it were in a moment we lost the sight, and withal our watch cried *the General was cast away*, which was too true. For in that moment the frigate was devoured and swallowed up by the sea.' (Hakluyt)

Two years after this disaster Sir Walter Ralegh, who had risen to favour at Court, obtained the Queen's permission to send out another expedition to America. The Queen refused to let Ralegh take command in person, and so the expedition sailed under Sir Richard Grenville, who took with him a hundred pioneers. The settlement was made on Roanoke Island, off the coast of what is now North Carolina. The colony was named Virginia, in honour of the queen. Sir Walter Ralegh

Virginia founded 1585

But it was not a success. Sir Francis Drake, returning from a plundering raid on the Spanish Main, called at the infant colony in 1586 and brought back all the colonists with him, at their own request. Next year Ralegh tried again and sent out another 150 colonists. Their fate is a mystery. When an English ship next visited the island, the colony was found to be abandoned. There was no sign of the colonists; they had simply disappeared, nor were they ever heard of again. They had probably all been massacred by the Indians. So ended the first attempt to plant an English colony overseas.

(iii) *Piracy and War.*

John Hawkins

Like the first English voyages to Russia, those to West Africa began in Mary's reign. Thomas Wyndham and John Lok made several expeditions to the Guinea Coast, in spite of the protests of the Portuguese government. Early in Elizabeth's reign the Portuguese monopoly was again infringed, this time by a greater man – John Hawkins. His methods were effective, though crude. He just landed on the Guinea Coast and seized 300 negroes. He had been told that

The Slave Trade

the negroes would be 'very good merchandise' in the West Indies, and so indeed he found. The Spanish colonists in America were very ready to buy Hawkins' human cargo, but the Spanish government, which forbade trade between its colonists and foreign nations, was seriously annoyed.

San Juan d'Ulloa 1567

Hawkins made two successful slave voyages (1562 and 1564), in the second of which the Queen's ship, the *Jesus of Lubeck*, took part. Then, on his third voyage (1567) he met with disaster. He obtained his 'merchandise' in Africa, sold it in the West Indies, and prepared to return home. With him was his young cousin, Francis Drake. A storm drove Hawkins' six ships on to the Mexican coast, and he sought shelter in the Spanish port of San Juan d'Ulloa. Scarcely had he done so when a Spanish fleet of thirteen vessels appeared outside the harbour. Hawkins seriously considered denying them entry, but, probably fearing the Queen's displeasure if he committed so hostile an act, he decided to let them come in. They gave a definite promise not to molest him; but six days later, reinforced by soldiers from the mainland, they suddenly attacked him. He lost the *Jesus* and three smaller vessels, but he got away on the *Minion*, crowded with 200 survivors. Drake also escaped with the remaining ship, the *Judith*. Hawkins decided to put 100 men ashore on the Mexican coast, since his ship could not carry so large a crew. These unfortunate sailors afterwards fell into the hands of the Spanish Inquisition. Some were burnt at the stake, some publicly flogged, some condemned to a lifetime of slavery in the galleys.

The incident of San Juan d'Ulloa made a great impression on Francis Drake. He detested the Spanish methods – their cruelty to captured Englishmen, no less than their refusal to trade on equal terms. Henceforth he made it his business, not to try to trade with the Spaniards, but to make war on them. In those days it was possible for a private subject to commit warlike acts against the subjects of another nation without necessarily involving his country in war. Drake's trade, in fact, was that of the privateer. It was no new thing; on the contrary, there had been privateers in European waters for many centuries. But no one, before or since, ever brought privateering to the same pitch of success as Francis Drake.

Francis Drake

In 1572 Drake sailed from Plymouth with two ships and made for the Gulf of Panama. He landed at Nombre de Dios and made friends with the natives. With their help he crossed the hills to a point where he would meet the Spanish mule train, laden with the silver of Peru, crossing the Isthmus of Panama from the Pacific to the Atlantic coast. The Englishmen fell on the oncoming mule-train, captured it, and brought off as much silver as they could carry away. Then they loaded their ships and made for home. It was during this expedition that Drake climbed the tree from which he could see the Atlantic and Pacific Oceans at the same time.

Drake's voyage round the world 1577-80

Five years later Drake sailed from Plymouth on his most famous voyage (1577). The Queen had taken shares in the expedition,

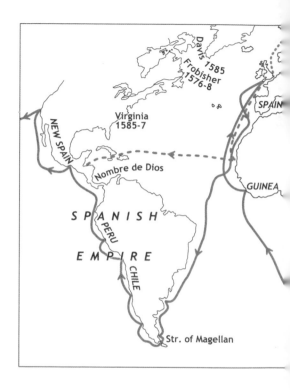

though, of course, she pretended to know nothing about it. He sailed for South America, and successfully navigated the dangerous Magellan Straits, though he lost four out of his five ships in doing so. With the remaining ship, the *Golden Hind*, he sailed up the Chilean coast, and proceeded to raid the principal Spanish ports. Lima and Valparaiso were plundered before the startled inhabitants realized that an English ship was in the Pacific. The *Golden Hind* was now laden with a cargo of gold and precious stones. Leaving the Spaniards behind, Drake sailed north (see map). He spent the winter in a land which he called New Albion, but which is now called California. From there, in the spring, the intrepid sailor set out across the

First English Voyage round the World (Drake)
- - - Direction of Slave Trade (Hawkins)
••••••• Expedition to Russia (Chacellor, Jenkinson)

THE ELIZABETHAN SEAMEN

unknown waters of the Pacific, until he reached the East Indies. He accomplished the difficult voyage through the islands, sailed across the Indian Ocean, and rounded the Cape. On 26 September 1580 he sailed into Plymouth Sound, having been absent rather less than three years. Drake was the first Englishman to sail round the world, a remarkable achievement when one remembers the lack of charts in those days.

The Spanish ambassador was extremely angry. Elizabeth invited him to accompany her to Deptford where Drake's ship was lying. She then gave a display of that cool courage – not to say insolence – which lay behind all her hesitation. She went on board the Golden

SIR FRANCIS DRAKE (1540-1596)
(Portrait c. 1590 by Marcus Geeraerts the Younger.)

Hind and knighted the arch-pirate in the presence of the Spanish
ambassador. Drake was allowed to keep £10,000 worth of his booty;
the promoters of the voyage took the rest, the Queen's share being
close on half a million.

Drake's raid
1585

Even after this the conflict with Spain was delayed another five
years. Then, in 1585, Philip laid an embargo on all English ships in
Spanish ports. Elizabeth decided to retaliate, and sent for Drake, who
was commissioned to undertake a raid on the Spanish colonies. He

sailed from Plymouth, with Frobisher as second in command, and made first for the Cape Verde Islands, where two towns were destroyed. He then crossed the Atlantic, burnt Santo Domingo, then seized Cartagena on the Spanish Main, and held it to ransom. Passing north to Florida, he burnt the town of St. Augustine, where not a single house was left standing. Then he returned home with a rich booty.

5. The Defeat of the Armada

Elizabeth had been reigning in England for thirty years before Philip sent his great Armada to attack her. The chief reason for this delay was that the King was not anxious to rush into a conflict, of which the result might be doubtful, and which would in any case involve considerable expense. There were, however, several reasons why Philip at last decided to resort to strong measures. The English sailors had, for over twenty years, been conducting piratical raids on Spanish ships and Spanish ports. The climax to all this was Drake's destructive raid on the West Indies (1585). The Pope was urging Philip to embark on a war which he regarded as a crusade to destroy a heretical government, though he was not the first Pope to do so. Above all, Elizabeth's interference in the Netherlands had become intolerable; since the Leicester expedition of 1586-7 her actions were no longer compatible with the existence of friendly relations.

The execution of Mary Queen of Scots (February 1587) removed whatever doubts remained in Philip's mind. He had always questioned the wisdom of placing Mary on the English throne, for Mary was French, not Spanish, by upbringing and sympathy. Besides this, her son, James VI of Scotland, who was presumably the heir to both kingdoms, was a Protestant. But Mary had, not long before her death, disinherited James and passed on her claims to the English throne to Philip himself. After that, Philip hesitated no longer. He gave orders for a great Armada to be prepared in all the ports of Spain.

Drifting into war

The raid on
Cadiz 1587

It was while these preparations were being made that Drake brought off another great raid. Commissioned by the Queen to reconnoitre the Spanish ports, he made straight for Cadíz, a major Spanish port. With characteristic boldness he left twenty of his twenty-four ships outside, and entered the harbour with only four vessels. But Drake's apparent rashness was grounded on confidence. He knew that the heavily armed ships of the type which Henry VIII had laid down, and which had been improved since, gave the English an immense advantage over the Spanish galleys defending Cadiz. These galleys depended on their power to ram and sink their opponent with their steel-shod beaks; they were no match against Drake's broadsides. As the galleys dashed towards him, he opened fire. A dreadful execution was done; the naked galley-slaves were mown down in hundreds, and it was impossible for the survivors to row towards the English ships. The victors of Lepanto[25] were beaten by a weapon against which they were powerless.

The result of this raid justified the boast of Fenner (Drake's friend) that twelve of Her Majesty's ships were a match for all the galleys in the King's service. But all his countrymen did not share Fenner's confidence. To many, perhaps to most, the danger seemed appalling. England was without allies, a small country, with no regular army, standing alone against the might of the greatest empire in the world, an empire on which, it was boasted, 'the sun never set'. Philip was the master of the New World, and of a considerable portion of the Old. By annexing Portugal (1580) he had absorbed the dominions of his only serious rival in America and the Indies. The famous Spanish infantry were thought to be unbeatable. And it was these very soldiers, commanded by one of the greatest generals in history – the Duke of Parma – who were waiting to invade England. No wonder Philip pushed forward his preparations to crush the insolent islanders.

---

[25] A great Spanish victory over the Turks in the Mediterranean (1571).

Philip's plan was to conquer England from the Netherlands, where Parma's army, 30,000 strong, was mustered. Parma built flat-bottomed boats at Antwerp in sufficient numbers to convey his army to England. When the Dutch blockaded the mouth of the Scheldt, he caused a canal to be dug, so that the boats could be moved to Dunkirk. But, as Parma well knew, to cross to England was impossible without a protecting fleet. It was for this purpose that the Armada was provided. It was hoped that a large Spanish fleet could dispose of a smaller number of English vessels, and that then the way would be clear for Parma to invade England. *The plan of invasion*

But this plan of invasion was never carried into effect, for the Spanish fleet, though roughly equal in numbers, was hopelessly inferior in every other respect. There were just over 130 ships in the Armada, but a large proportion were merchant vessels, commandeered for war, originating from many parts of Europe, and with crews whose commitment to the cause was doubtful. Their guns were light and badly placed, because the Spaniards lacked a suitable arms industry. Thus armed, the famous Spanish galleons were not much more fit to encounter the English ships, armed with guns of superior range than were the oared galleys which Drake had destroyed in Cadíz harbour. The Spanish object, however, was not to crush the English fleet, but to brush it aside so that an invasion of England could proceed. That is why the Armada carried 18,000 soldiers, who were to help Parma's army, and only 8,000 sailors. The commander of the Armada was the Duke of Medina Sidonia, a man who was no sailor, but was an experienced naval administrator. He also had the advantage of being one of the first grandees of Spain, when high rank was essential in a commander to get the lesser officers, nobles themselves, to obey orders. Medina Sidonia was not hopeful of Spanish success, but their defeat was certainly not due to his incompetence. *The Spanish Armada 1588*

The English fleet differed in several important respects from the Armada. In the first place, the thirty-four vessels belonging to the *The English Fleet*

Queen were real ships of war. They were all heavily armed with guns, and in this respect each of the Queen's ships was vastly superior to any Spanish ship afloat. They had all been carefully put in order by John Hawkins. The only defects of the English fleet – and they were serious enough – were a shortage of powder and a shortage of food; the shortage of powder was partly due to the unexpectedly large quantity used during the action, and the shortage of food was the fault of the system of victualling. In addition to the ships of the Royal Navy, some fifty or more privately owned vessels joined in the fight; these ships also were much better armed than the corresponding vessels in the Armada.

But besides their superiority in gun-power, the English had another advantage: their ships were manned by fighting sailors, trained in the school of Hawkins and Drake. The supreme command, it is true, was given to Lord Howard of Effingham, and he, like Medina Sidonia, was chosen for his rank. But the other officers were men like Drake, Hawkins, Frobisher, and others whose names the Spaniards had already learnt to dread.

The Armada sails in the Channel

The Armada entered the English Channel on Saturday, 20 July 1588. The Spaniards saw no signs of their enemy. But the next morning, when they were off Plymouth, sixty English ships attacked them in a manner to which they could not respond. Instead of closing with the enemy, in the traditional style, the English passed by the Spanish fleet, each ship firing, as it passed, a terrific broadside. The Spaniards could not reply, for, with their inadequate guns, they were out of range. Nor could they close with the enemy, for the English sailed away.

Off Calais

All that week the entire Armada moved slowly up-Channel; there were two minor fights off the Dorset coast and the Isle of Wight. Yet the English attacks seemed to achieve little: the Spaniards had suffered little damage and had maintained their formation. The English fleet was running critically short of ammunition. On

Saturday, 27 July, a week after they had entered the Channel, the Spaniards dropped anchor in Calais Roads. Here Medina Sidonia sent a message to Parma, and perhaps intended waiting for him. But he was not allowed to do so. Drake, taking advantage of a favourable wind, sent fire-ships among the Spanish fleet. No ship was actually set on fire, but they all panicked, cut their cables and made for the open sea. The Spaniards were driven from Calais, their formation gone.

On Monday, 29 July, was fought the battle of Gravelines. The wind again favoured the English, for it blew strongly towards the Flemish coast, from which the Spaniards struggled to get away. As they did so, broadside after broadside from the English guns battered their ships and cut down their soldiers. It was a terrible slaughter; and the Spaniards, as at Plymouth, could make no effective reply from their own feeble guns. Only a lucky change in the direction of the wind saved the Spaniards from being driven upon the sandbanks of Flanders. Though they lost only two or three ships at Gravelines, the whole fleet was badly damaged – how badly was shown in the sequel. For Medina Sidonia, recognizing defeat, was forced by the wind to sail round Great Britain and make for Ireland – a friendly Catholic country, as he thought. But his ships, battered by the English guns at Gravelines, were in no condition to make so long a voyage. All leaked badly, they were short of food and water, a great storm arose, and there were no friendly harbours in England or Scotland. Soon many of the ships became wrecks. Many of them were driven on to the inhospitable shores of Scotland and Ireland. Of the 130 ships which had made up the Armada, only half reached home, and the toll taken on the men was even worse: perhaps 60 per cent perished.

Battle of Gravelines 29 July

The end of the Armada

6. The Last Years of Elizabeth

The English naval war with Spain (1588-1604) did not end till after Elizabeth's death. To pursue it vigorously was contrary to all the Queen's instincts; besides, she rightly remembered that war is very costly. But, in the first flush of the victory over the Armada, the war party, led by Walsingham and Drake, was in the ascendant. Early in 1589, therefore, the offensive was taken against Spain. It was arranged that an English naval force should first destroy the remains of the Armada in the north Spanish ports and then land an army in Portugal to assist Dom Antonio (the Portuguese pretender) to gain the throne and expel the Spaniards from his country. An English Armada, larger than the Spanish Armada, was assembled under Drake; on board was an army of about 19,000 men. The expedition sailed, landed at Corunna and sacked the town, then went on towards Lisbon. But Drake failed to force the passage of the Tagus, and the army, owing to its lack of siege-guns, was repulsed from Lisbon with some slight loss. There was no sign of the expected Portuguese rising on behalf of Dom Antonio. After a vain attempt to capture the Spanish treasure fleet and ignoring their orders to destroy the remains of the Armada, the English Armada returned home.

Expedition to Portugal 1589

Elizabeth was extremely angry: England had lost 11,000 men, largely to sickness, and she had lost all the money she had invested in the expedition. Drake was in disgrace for the next five years, during which time little was attempted at sea beyond raids against Spanish treasure-ships. In 1591 Admiral Lord Thomas Howard was sent to the Azores, with Sir Richard Grenville as second in command. Arrived there, the Admiral learnt that the Spaniards had mustered a large battle fleet to escort their treasure-ships home. He wisely decided to retreat, as he was completely outnumbered. Sir Richard Grenville, however, in the *Revenge*, remained – to wage his immortal fight with one ship against the whole Spanish fleet. So formidable were the English guns that the *Revenge* put up a fight lasting a day

Last fight of the 1591

THE NAVAL WAR 1585-1604

and a night before she surrendered. Then a storm arose which sank the *Revenge* together with over a hundred of the enemy warships and treasure-ships.

Meanwhile, the battle of politics was being fought at home. There is scarcely any period in English history which can boast of a more brilliant group of men than those who moved in the Court of Elizabeth during her last decade. The elderly Queen, still expecting – and receiving – the flattery and attention to which she had been accustomed for nearly forty years, was the goddess of that Court. The brilliant Sir Walter Ralegh was being superseded by Essex, a new

Essex

favourite. Robert Devereux, Earl of Essex, was a member of the old nobility of England. Young, handsome, and proud, bold to the point of recklessness, Essex exerted a strange fascination over the ageing Queen. He was about twenty-one when he succeeded his step-father Leicester (who died in 1588) as the first of the queen's courtiers: she was fifty-five. Though Elizabeth was flattered by the attentions of so young a cavalier, she was far too old a diplomatist to allow him, as he desired, to influence her policy. Her chief minister was the man who had stood by her side for forty years, Lord Burghley, now seventy years of age. He was getting feeble and gouty; but his son, the clever hunchback, Sir Robert Cecil, was ready to take his place. Against the Cecils stood Essex, the dazzling earl who sought the overthrow of the 'old fox', as he called Burghley.

Death of
Hawkins
and Drake
1595-6

The years 1595-7 saw a vigorous revival of the prosecution of the Spanish war. Elizabeth, alarmed at the news that Philip was preparing another Armada, sent once more for her old sailors. Hawkins and Drake undertook a raid on the Spanish possessions in the West Indies (1595), but it was a failure. As he once more sailed his ship on Nombre de Dios Bay, Drake found that the Spaniards were considerably stronger than in the great days of his youth. Hawkins died at sea, and soon afterwards Drake himself died of a sickness which had already carried off large numbers of his men. He was buried at sea, in the waters that washed the Spanish Main, where his name had been a word of terror for a generation.

The next year another fleet sailed from England under Lord Howard of Effingham, Lord Thomas Howard, and Sir Walter Ralegh. Essex commanded the army of 8,000 men which it carried. This fleet destroyed the shipping in Cadíz harbour; Essex and his men landed and took the town, which they gave to the flames. Philip swore vengeance, and, against the advice of his captains, dispatched another Armada to England in the late autumn (1596). It was, however, destroyed by a storm and never even sighted the English

ELIZABETHAN COSTUME

(From a book published in 1581.) From left to right are: (1) the rich London merchant, (2) a noblewoman, (3) an ordinary housewife in her best dress and (4) a 'plebeian young man'.

ELIZABETHAN ARCHITECTURE:

A typical large country house of the period. Notice the wings projecting at each end, and the square mullioned windows. (Montacute House, Somerset, from a water-colour by J.C. Buckler.)

137

coast. The next year Essex and Ralegh went off on the 'Islands Voyage' – to the Azores. They missed the Spanish treasure-fleet by a few hours, quarrelled bitterly, and returned home empty-handed to face a wrathful Queen. By way of reply, Philip, who was now a dying man, ordered a third Armada to sail, but it suffered the same fate as its predecessor.

The Islands Voyage 1597

The Islands Voyage was the last effort of the war as far as Elizabeth was concerned, though English privateers continued to attack Spanish merchant ships. The damage they did was considerable, and the main Spanish fleet from America could only cross the Atlantic with a large convoy of warships. Philip II died in 1598, passing on to his successor the unsolved problem of the conquest of England. That same year Elizabeth lost her old servant Burghley, whom she comforted in his last illness.

Death of Philip II 1598

The hopes of the Spaniards were now centred on Ireland, where the population was in a constant state of rebellion against the English government. In an evil hour, Essex persuaded the queen to let him lead an expedition for the conquest of Ireland (1599). But once arrived there, he did nothing except make a truce with the Earl of Tyrone, the chief rebel, which he was not authorized to do. Then he suddenly came home, leaving his army behind. For thus disobeying his instructions and deserting his post he was utterly disgraced. He was sentenced to lose all his offices and to be imprisoned in his own house. But the fiery earl was not the man to sit down under such treatment. He was still popular, and, imagining that he could overthrow the Government, he attempted to enlist the support of the London mob on his side; his rebellion, however, was a complete fiasco. For such behaviour there could be only one punishment, and Elizabeth signed his death warrant. Essex was only thirty-four at the time of his execution (February 1601).

Essex in Ireland 1599

His rebellion and death 1601

The glamour went out of the Court when Essex died. The wily Sir Robert Cecil was now the chief figure; and he was quietly preparing for the future – that future in which Elizabeth could have no part. No one dared mention the subject of her successor to the old Queen; but the careful Sir Robert was in secret communication with King James of Scotland, and all was ready for his peaceful accession to the English throne.

In 1601 Elizabeth attended her last Parliament. The chief grievance of the Commons was the question of monopolies, which meant the sole right to sell various articles; such rights were often granted to favoured subjects, like the late Earl of Essex. Such profiteering at the public expense was an obvious evil; Elizabeth saw that it would be prudent to give way. She sent a message to Parliament saying she would remedy the matter; the Commons replied, in the usual language of the day, that words could not express their gratitude, but 'in all duty and thankfulness, prostrate at your feet, we present our most loyal and thankful hearts ... and the last spirit of breath in our nostrils, to be poured out, to be breathed up, for your safety'.

Elizabeth's last Parliament

The Queen took the opportunity of making a noble speech; the members knelt as she addressed them.

'There is no jewel, be it of never so rich a price, which I prefer before this jewel, I mean your love. For I do more esteem it than any treasure or riches; for that we know how to prize, but love and thanks I count inestimable. And though God hath raised me high, yet this I count the glory of my Crown, that I have reigned with your loves ... There will never queen sit in my seat with more zeal to my country, or more care to my subjects, and that will sooner with willingness yield and venture her life for your good and safety than myself. And though you have had, and may have, many Princes more mighty and wise sitting in this seat, yet you never had, or shall have, any that will be more careful and loving.'

7. The Puritans

The severity of the laws against Popish recusants was not relaxed during Elizabeth's reign. On the contrary, a further disability was inflicted on them by an Act of 1593. This Act began by a reference to 'sundry wicked and seditious persons, terming themselves Catholics, and being indeed spies and intelligencers for her Majesty's foreign enemies'. It went on to say that all Popish recusants would in future be forbidden to travel more than five miles from their homes. The intention was obviously to hinder the work of possible plotters. But the suspicion was the more ungenerous, for the main body of English Catholics had shown themselves loyal subjects since the attempted Spanish invasion of 1588.

But during the latter part of Elizabeth's reign the main question with which the Anglican bishops were concerned was the spread of Puritan ideas. The Puritans were those who were dissatisfied with the Church settlement of 1559. They desired a purer (i.e. simpler) form of worship – they considered the Anglican service was still too much like the Roman – and they set great store by strictness of conduct. Above all, they aimed to secure full inward commitment to the Protestant religion among the people, not merely outward conformity to it.

Many of the clergy favoured the Puritan ideas, and the movement gained ground in many parts of the country. Thomas Cartwright,
Cartwright who had been Professor of Divinity at Cambridge, was one of the Puritan leaders. He was much influenced by the teaching of Calvin, who had advocated Church government by presbyters or elders and ministers instead of by bishops. Cartwright believed in godly discipline for the congregation and he held that the Presbyterian system could better achieve this. Elizabeth was determined to uphold the authority of bishops, since it was through them that she ruled the Church. In the 1570s she became alarmed by the 'prophesyings', meetings of local clergy for prayer and discussion. She believed that

these meetings might undercut the authority of the bishops, but her Archbishop of Canterbury, Edmund Grindal, refused to suppress them, since in his view they could help to improve the knowledge and understanding of the clergy. Grindal was suspended from his office in 1577. When he died in 1583, the Queen appointed a disciplinarian called John Whitgift as Archbishop of Canterbury. Though Calvinist in many of his doctrines, he was determined to root out Presbyterian ideas and tried to impose upon the clergy acceptance of everything in the Prayer Book of 1559 as well as the wearing of the surplice, seen by Puritans as too similar to the vestments worn by Catholic priests. Whitgift did destroy Presbyterianism as a concerted movement, but he never achieved total conformity with his wishes, since moderate Puritans had too much support from influential lords and gentry.

Whitgift attempted to check the spread of the obnoxious doctrines by establishing a strict censorship of the Press, under the control of the Bishop of London and himself. But the Puritan leaders were too clever for him. In 1588 they set up secret printing presses in out-of-the-way parts of the country, and distributed pamphlets, all bearing the signature 'Martin Mar-prelate'. The pamphlets contained an attack, not only on the office of bishop, but on the personal character of the individual bishops of the Anglican Church. The most scurrilous terms of abuse were employed. Whitgift and his colleagues were stung by this insidious attack, but they found it difficult to stamp it out, since they could not trace its source. Still, the pamphlets were so subversive that it is doubtful whether they really assisted the Puritan cause.

Elizabeth's Church was rejected by Robert Browne (c.1550-1633), who graduated at Cambridge and founded a church at Norwich on what were later known as Congregational principles. He did not believe that there should be a national, state-run Church at all, but rather that voluntary and independent congregations should control their own religious life. In view of their hostility to any state

Archbishop
Whitgift
1583-1604

Martin
Mar-prelate

Browne

141

Church, these people were regarded as particularly dangerous. Therefore in 1593 a Statute directed against separatists (so-called because they wished to separate themselves from the national Church) was passed through Parliament. This Act devised severe penalties for the frequenters of unauthorised religious meetings; imprisonment, banishment from the realm, and even the death penalty were included as possible punishments. The result was persecution A few separatists were actually put to death; many more fled to Holland, there to form congregations of Englishmen who, in the next generation became the nucleus of the New England beyond the seas.

In that age moderation in either politics or religion was rare. Only a very exceptional mind, such as that of Francis Bacon, a nephew of Lord Burghley, could see the follies of both sides. In his *Advertisement touching the Controversies of the Church of England* (1589) Bacon pointed to the extravagance of the Puritans, their absurd distrust of almost all former doctrines and practices, and their indecent and libellous style of writing. On the other hand, he censured the Anglican bishops for their persecuting spirit. He told them that if they insisted too strongly on uniformity among English Protestants they would make themselves ridiculous in the eyes of the world, by exhibiting a Church divided against itself. For Bacon saw, what Whitgift could not see, that persecution can stimulate the thing which it is designed to suppress. Neither Whitgift nor Queen Elizabeth realized how deeply Puritan views had taken root. Nor could they foresee that the controversy, bitter as it was in their time, would help to produce the civil war of the following century.

In the beginning of the year 1603, when she was seventy years old, Elizabeth's vigour began to fail. In March she died after a short illness. Cecil had already arranged for the accession of the King of Scotland, which took place without any disturbance. It is very likely that most English people welcomed the end of the Elizabethan era. The Queen's last years had been marred by a series of terrible

Francis Bacon on persecution

Death of Elizabeth March 1603

harvests, by widespread hardship among the people, by heavy taxes, by lack of success in the war with Spain, and by struggles at court which got out of hand with the rebellion of Essex. The Queen herself was losing the glamour she had once possessed. It was the disasters of the Stuart period which created nostalgia for the Queen's reign and caused the view that it had been a golden age to take root.

Date Summary: Elizabeth
(1558-1603)

ENGLAND, SCOTLAND AND IRELAND	EUROPE, ASIA AND AMERICA

THE YEARS OF PEACE

1559 Acts of Uniformity and Supremacy	1559 Jenkinson in Moscow
1560 Treaty of Edinburgh	
	1562 Hawkins – Slave Trade
1563 Stat. Artificers	
1564 Birth of SHAKESPEARE	
1565 Mary Queen of Scots *m.* Darnley	
1567 Fall of Mary	1567 San Juan'd'Ulloa
	1570 Elizabeth excommunicated
1571 Ridolfi Plot	
1572 Norfolk executed	1572 Massacre of St. Bartholomew
	1576-8 Frobisher's Voyages
	1577-80 DRAKE round the World
1579-83 Munster Rebellion	
1581 Campion executed	
1583 Whitgift Archbishop	1583 Gilbert (Newfoundland)
	1584 William of Orange murdered

THE SPANISH WAR

	1585 Drake's Raid-America
1587 Mary Queen of Scots executed	1587 Drake's Raid—Cadíz
1588 SPANISH ARMADA	
	1591-4 Lancaster's Voyage
	1591 The *Revenge*
1593 Act against Puritans	
Marlowe died	
1595-1603 Tyrone's Rebellion	
	1596 Drake *d*.
	1597 'Islands Voyage'
	1598 Philip II of Spain died
	1600 East India Company
1601 POOR LAW CODE	

VI

THE AGE OF SHAKESPEARE

1. The Poets and the Drama

ELIZABETHAN England, 'a nest of singing birds', was famous for its love of music. The lute, the viol (forerunner of the violin), and the virginals (forerunner of the piano) were the favourite instruments. English composers were known throughout Europe; Tallis (*d*. 1585) and his pupil Byrd (*d*. 1623) and Orlando Gibbons (*d*. 1625) all excelled in the field of sacred music. Of these Byrd enjoyed a reputation in the musical world comparable with that of Shakespeare in the world of letters.

English Music

The opening lines of *Twelfth Night* – 'If music be the food of love, play on' – are spoken by a love-sick lord surrounded by his musicians, and remind us that the ordinary attendants of every man of wealth included minstrels and singers. 'Let music sound while he doth make his choice', says Portia in the casket scene in the *Merchant of Venice*, the play in which Shakespeare has given his noble estimate of the power of music:

> The man that hath no music in himself,
> Nor is not mov'd with concord of sweet sounds,
> Is fit for treasons, stratagems and spoils.

Singing and dancing, too, were much in fashion in Tudor times; and in the modern revival of Folk and Morris dances we can hear again the jolly tunes of Shakespeare's England.

and songs

Moreover, the Elizabethan Age, so rich in music, also produced some of the greatest lyric poets (i.e. song writers) in any literature. Shakespeare himself wrote some of the best English songs: '0 Mistress Mine', 'Where the bee sucks there suck I', 'Who is Sylvia?',

'Sigh no more, ladies', 'Under the greenwood tree', 'Blow, blow, thou winter wind'. His contemporary, Ben Jonson (1573-1637) wrote many lyrics including the famous 'Drink to me only with thine eyes'; while in Thomas Ford's *Music of Sundry Kinds* (1607) appeared the equally well-known 'There is a lady sweet and kind', by an anonymous writer. Robert Herrick, a Devonshire clergyman who lived under the Stuart kings, but who carried on the Elizabethan lyric tradition, wrote: 'Cherry Ripe', 'Corinna's gone a-Maying', 'Gather ye rosebuds while ye may', and the exquisite

> Fair Daffodils, we weep to see
> You haste away so soon ...

Edmund
Spenser

The Elizabethan Age of English poetry filled the last two decades of the Queen's reign and overlapped into that of her successor. The earliest Elizabethan poets, Sir Philip Sidney and Edmund Spenser, both produced poetry which was of great merit. Spenser loved to wander in the realms of medieval fancy. If he spoke of war, he thought of knights in shining armour; if of peace, of shepherds and shepherdesses living in idyllic happiness. Spenser's longest poem, *The Faerie Queene*, is an elaborate allegory; his Red Cross Knight is Holiness, his Sir Guyon, Temperance, and so on. Some of the characters represent historical personages. The 'faln Duessa' is perhaps Mary Queen of Scots and the Wizard Archimago Philip of Spain; Gloriana, the Queen of the Faerie Court ('That greatest Glorious Queene of Faeryland'), is, of course, Queen Elizabeth, for whom no flattery could be too gross in the eyes of the court poets.

Far different from this elaborate and at times artificial verse of the Court was the bold, new dramatic art, which was at the same time coming into popular favour. English drama had grown up out of the old Miracle and Morality Plays which were performed during the Middle Ages in all the chief English towns, usually by the guildsmen. English acting for long retained the simple and direct character of

THE TITLE PAGE OF SHAKESPEARE'S FIRST FOLIO,
published in 1623 shortly after the Bard's death in 1616.

these early performances, designed to appeal to the rough humour and passions of the common folk; but the plays themselves gradually lost their religious basis. In Elizabeth's day university men began to write plays of a non-religious character, which soon became popular, especially in London. These men – Peele, Greene, Nash, and Marlowe – were the forerunners of Shakespeare.

Marlowe
Christopher Marlowe (1564-93) was born in the same year as Shakespeare and was killed in a tavern brawl before he was thirty. His best plays had a considerable influence on the work of Shakespeare. Marlowe's Jew is the precursor of Shylock; his Edward II resembles Shakespeare's Richard II. Marlowe first made use of a blank verse rhythm which soon became the recognized medium for the drama. His style is rich and rhetorical; some of his plays contain lines of great beauty, as in the passage when Faustus (who has sold his soul to the Devil) beholds the face of Helen of Troy:

> Is this the face that launched a thousand ships
> And burnt the topless towers of Ilium?
> Sweet Helen, make me immortal with a kiss.

Shakespeare
The university playwrights, of whom Marlowe was the greatest, were overshadowed by a young man from the country, who had been educated at a grammar school. William Shakespeare (1564-1616) was the son of a tradesman of Stratford-on-Avon, and went to the old guild-school of that town, which had been recently re-founded as King Edward VI's Grammar School. He worked with his father, married, and had three children. He was still under thirty when he
The London Theatre
came up to London to make his fortune – perhaps a year or two before the defeat of the Armada.

Shakespeare began his connexion with the theatre as an actor; but after a time he was employed in writing up parts for his fellow performers. When he first came to town, most plays were performed in the courtyards of inns, which had galleries running round, in which the wealthier spectators paid to sit; other people stood in the 'pit' or ground of the inn-yard. But during Elizabeth's reign several covered-in theatres were built. It seems strange to think that these theatres were only allowed on sufferance; the city authorities regarded plays as opportunities for rowdyism and gatherings of the mob. It was for this reason that the first theatres were built in the suburbs, like Southwark and Shoreditch. There was practically no scenery; changes of place were indicated by a written notice, such as: 'Scene: A Rocky Coast.' The actors wore costume, but otherwise they had no artificial aid to their performance, and there were no women players.

Shakespeare's first play was probably *Love's Labour's Lost*, a satire on the affected court speech of the time. *Romeo and Juliet* was another early play, and was followed by the three parts of *Henry VI* (not all Shakespeare), *Richard II*, *Richard III*, and *King John*, all of which owe something to the influence of Marlowe. The comedies, such as *The Merchant of Venice*, *A Midsummer-Night's Dream*, *Twelfth Night*, and *As You Like It*, belong to the middle period of Shakespeare's writing life, as do the two parts of *Henry IV* and *Henry V.* The wonderful series of tragedies was written in the decade 1599-1609; for then appeared *Julius Caesar*, *Hamlet*, *Othello*, *Macbeth*, *King Lear*, and *Antony and Cleopatra*. In his latter years the note of tragedy was softened, and Shakespeare closed his active life with the writing of *Cymbeline*, *A Winter's Tale*, and *The Tempest*. {Shakespeare's Plays}

It is needless to say that Shakespeare's leading characters – Hamlet, Lear, Othello, Lady Macbeth, Shylock, or Falstaff – are among the finest productions of human genius. The problems with which the soul of Hamlet was tormented draw men's sympathy as much to-day as they did three hundred years ago; the tragedy of Lear or of Macbeth is still as haunting. To this supreme quality of the creation of character Shakespeare added a grandeur of poetic language never excelled in English. The deaths of his greatest characters called forth some of the poet's noblest lines, as in the famous 'To-morrow and to-morrow and to-morrow' speech spoken by Macbeth on the death of his queen;[26] in the great speeches pronounced by Antony over Caesar's murdered corpse;[27] or in the beautiful lines spoken by Cleopatra over the body of the dead Antony.[28]

His debt to nature

Whatever lessons Shakespeare may have learnt about human character in the rough-and-tumble London world of theatre and tavern, he never lost the memories of his native Warwickshire. It was from there that he drew his sweetest images from the flowers that grew in the Stratford lanes and from the trees and glades of the forest of Arden, which his imagination peopled with elves and fairies. The bank

> whereon the wild thyme blows,
> Where oxlips and the nodding violet grows

which the Fairy King remembered, his creator remembered too. Again and again in many beautiful lines he called to mind the flowering fields of his boyhood. And the lovely scenes in *A Midsummer-Night's Dream* and *As You Like It* owe their origin to the poet's early wanderings in the groves of Arden.

Shakespeare seems to have been curiously uninterested in the main political and religious problems of Tudor history. The great religious controversy of Catholic and Protestant is passed over in silence. We may judge, however, that the poet disliked the bigoted reformers, from the fact that he held up the Puritanical Malvolio to a scorn and ridicule from which nothing can ever rescue him. 'Dost thou think, because thou art virtuous, there shall be no more cakes and ale?' asks the drunken Sir Toby. The champion of cakes and ale is sympathetically drawn; the shocked Malvolio is not.

---

[26] *Macbeth*, Act v, Scene v.
[27] *Julius Caesar*, Act III, Scenes i and ii.
[28] *Antony and Cleopatra*, Act IV, Scene xiii.

It has often been remarked that Shakespeare wrote King John without mentioning Magna Carta; and it is indeed probable that historical problems, as such, did not interest him. His historical personages, like Richard II and III, Henry IV and V, Julius Caesar and Antony, are interesting merely as characters, not on account of their political importance. No one, for example, would gather from reading *Julius Caesar* how great a part Caesar payed in the world's history. But in one respect Shakespeare, like all Elizabethans, was politically minded: he was intensely patriotic. The conscious pride of the nation which had humbled the might of Spain breathes in the bombastic words which Shakespeare puts into the mouth of Henry V, or of Falconbridge, in *King John*: His patriotism

> Come the three corners of the world in arms,
> And we shall shock them. Nought shall make us rue,
> If England to itself do rest but true.

and even in the softer words of Gaunt in *Richard II*, which bespeak a real love of England:

> This royal throne of kings, this sceptred isle,
> This earth of majesty, this seat of Mars,
> This other Eden, demi-paradise,
> This fortress built by Nature for herself
> Against infection and the hand of war ...

Shakespeare wrote for all ages, and his greatest characters can never lose their appeal. But his plays are also the mirror of his own time. Elizabethan England was an aristocratic society, and the lords and ladies who are the chief characters in most of Shakespeare's plays were real enough to him. It was then natural that an actor and playwright should portray an aristocratic society; for upon the favour of these lords the very existence of an actor depended. It was at the numerous festivities at their castles and halls that the strolling players had a welcome; even in London, certain noblemen, like Lord Southampton, Shakespeare's friend, protected the actors. 'Good my lord,' says Hamlet to Polonius, 'will you see the players well bestowed? Do you hear, let them be well used.'

2. Social and Industrial Changes

A brilliant age

In order to see the Elizabethan Age as a whole we must look at both sides of the picture, and see both the brilliance and the squalor. The brilliance is obvious enough: a national Church founded, a great tradition of drama created, a powerful enemy defeated, the globe circumnavigated. And never, perhaps, in English history, have the habits of the upper classes of society improved so rapidly as in the century between the battle of Bosworth and the Spanish Armada. It is indeed a far cry from the bullying barons who intimidated local juries under Henry VI or who rode up and down England in the armies of York and Lancaster, to the polished courtiers of Queen Elizabeth. And yet, underneath the brilliant surface, perhaps the savage was not so very deeply buried. Those smart men of fashion, with their music and their poetry, their silks and satins and perfumes, could see dogs mauled by a bear or beggars whipped without a qualm, and 'the curious society which loved such fantasies and delicacies – how readily would it turn and rend a random victim with hideous cruelty!'[29]

The upper classes

Great material progress was made by the upper classes and the merchants in the Elizabethan Age. The aristocracy lived on the fat of the land. Lord Leicester turned Kenilworth Castle from a fortress into a palace; and the Great Lake which had once acted as a defence

---

[29] Lytton Strachey, *Elizabeth and Essex*.

to that castle became a pleasure lake, where boats filled with gaily clad minstrels sang the praises of Gloriana, the Queen. The change was typical of the times. With the peace that the Tudors brought after the Wars of the Roses, the day of the castle-fortress was happily past, and the 'great houses' of England were now being built. Charlecote House, Warwickshire – in the grounds of which, tradition says, the boy Shakespeare poached – was built in the first year of Elizabeth's reign. Many others followed, for the successful merchants and newly ennobled lords required homes suitable to their new magnificence.[30]

Next in rank to the nobility came the country squires. They were increasingly likely to have been educated at one of the two universities and to have picked up at least a smattering of law at the Inns of Court in London. By the end of Elizabeth's time, they were no longer inclined to pursue their quarrels by violence, but used the lawcourts instead. Even so, many of them still spent much of their time in hunting the deer or the hare. But they had very important functions to perform, for it was from the squires that the Justices of the Peace were drawn. These unpaid magistrates, whose office had been developing ever since the time of Edward III, managed the whole of the local government of England. Without their aid the government of the country could not have been carried on for a single month. They acted, as JPs still do, as magistrates administering local justice individually and in Quarter Sessions; but in addition the government loaded them with many other duties: they fixed wages; they saw to the upkeep of the roads; they licensed inns; and they oversaw the operation of the Poor Laws. Their work was controlled by the queen's Privy

Justices of the Peace

---

[30] Longleat House, Wiltshire; Burghley House and Castle Ashby, Northants.; Montacute House, Somerset (see illustration on p. 137); Bramhall Hall, Cheshire, and Wollaton Hall, Notts., are among the best known.

Council,[31] which enforced the laws passed by Parliament.

The merchants

The merchant class was closely concerned with the new England that was shaping. London was incomparably the greatest city in England, and the chief centre of trade; its population was multiplied five times in the century following the birth of Elizabeth. Sir Thomas Gresham, a famous merchant, built the Royal Exchange, and also helped Cecil in the difficult task of improving the coinage. Merchants still hoped, however, to use their wealth to purchase a landed estate and set up as a country gentleman.

The merchants of London, and to a lesser extent those of Bristol, were the mainstay of England's overseas trade. Medieval and Tudor ideas of business demanded that when a merchant traded with foreign lands he should do so as a member of a company, and before a company could trade it must have a royal charter. Foreign trade was often a dangerous business, and the merchants had to arm their ships – hence some sort of regulation, such as a charter conferred, was necessary to give authority to the company. The company was the descendant of the medieval Guild; and, like the Guild, it was jealous of all 'interlopers', that is, those unlicensed persons who dared to infringe a company's monopoly. In the earlier 'regulated' companies, like the Merchant Adventurers, each merchant used his own separate capital and made his own profit or loss. But the later type of company

Trading companies

traded on a joint stock; that is, the capital and the profits were pooled, and the stock-holders traded as a single firm, as is usual in modern business. The practice of pooling their capital enabled merchants to make longer voyages in larger ships. Thus they could attempt far larger enterprises than was possible with the older companies, and

---

[31] The Council, not the Parliament, was the real pivot of Tudor government. We are still reminded of this fact by Cranmer's Prayer Book (1549), wherein we are bidden to pray for 'the Lords of the Council' and the 'Magistrates' – but a prayer for the High Court of Parliament' was not made a regular part of the Church service till 1662 (after the Puritan Revolution).

take risks which were too serious for single merchants to bear. An early example of a joint-stock company was the Muscovy Company (1553), but the most remarkable was the East India Company (1600) – and these were the forerunners of numerous trading companies that gradually gave England a world-wide commerce.

The industrial life of Tudor England was greatly enriched by Protestant refugees from the Continent, who brought new industries and craft secrets with them. The Dutch and Walloon settlers in East Anglia taught the 'New Draperies' – the making of fine cloth such as 'baize' – to Englishmen, while Huguenot (French Protestant) settlers showed them how to make fine linen and silk.

Further, the growth of many new non-textile industries (coal, brass, salt, &c.) was so noticeable that the period 1550-1625 has been described as 'an early industrial revolution'. In fact England, which in 1550 had hardly any real industries except the cloth manufacture, was by 1625 almost industrially self-sufficing, though most of these new industries were very small.

The great majority of the English nation, however – probably The Yeoman more than five-sixths – was still engaged in rural pursuits. The prosperous yeomen owned and farmed their own land, and were the backbone of the country. Many of them became literate in the course of the 16th century and were attracted by the Puritan stress on a Bible-reading laity who took their religion seriously. Their importance was expressed in their undertaking of roles such as churchwarden and overseer of the poor.

Below the yeomen were the peasants, the largest class and mostly illiterate. Contemporaries supposed that many peasants had been reduced to poverty by enclosure, but in fact enclosure affected only certain areas of the country and even there was not on a huge scale. It seems that the poverty which was so great a problem was largely the product of a large increase in population from around two and a quarter million in 1525 to over four millions by 1603. Numbers increased much more rapidly than jobs, which led to an increase in unemployment and underemployment. The population also outran the growth of the food supply, which caused large rises in prices and therefore hardship for the poor.

Industrial and rural England in the Tudor Age were not two areas sharply divided off from each other, as they are at the present day. The men, women ('spinsters'), and children who worked for the wool merchant generally worked in their own cottages. This 'domestic system', as it has been called, lasted until the invention of mechanical spindles (in the eighteenth century) gradually made the cottage industry obsolete. It is difficult today to picture a country in which the

Village
industries

most important needs of life, such as food, housing, and clothing, were largely provided by the labour of each village. But there are a few places left in England where, if the old conditions have gone, we can still see the houses very much as they were in Tudor times. In East Anglia, in the Cotswolds, in the valleys of Wiltshire, and in the more remote of the Yorkshire dales (like Swaledale), farm and cottage, sturdily built of the local stone, look much the same as they did 300 years ago. But the cottage spinners and weavers who once inhabited them have long gone.

Changing
conditions

In the Tudor Age the world was changing rapidly. In England there were three main factors (decay of guilds, the increase of population, unemployment) which tended to upset the old order of things. The old guild system of industry was breaking down, and newer methods were developing. Competition was taking the place of custom. The Tudor epoch was a transition stage between the old guild system with its independent handicraftsmen and the factory with massed 'hands'. A class of 'captains of industry' – like the clothiers or drapers – was developing home industries on capitalist lines. Old and new industries were settling in villages and in the unchartered towns which were free from the old guild rules – such as Manchester, Sheffield, Leeds, and Birmingham. These and other places in Tudor times were still half village, half town. Yet at that time 'both in wealth and population Lavenham (the Suffolk wool town) was far more important than Birmingham. If any traveller in the 16th century had compared the mansion of the Springs (the wealthiest of the local clothiers), the fine houses of other manufacturers, the magnificent church, the great warehouses in Lavenham, with the broken-down manor house, the undistinguished church, the modest dwellings, the little tanneries and forges of Birmingham, and if he had been asked which of these two places was likely to become the second city in England, can we doubt that he would have chosen the flourishing seat of the greatest manufacture in the country?'[32]

The people of Tudor England suffered what we should now call an 'economic crisis'. Times were hard for those who suffered by the changes of the century. The government was compelled to legislate for the whole economic sphere of life, and this was one aspect of the growing scope of national government. In the Middle Ages the town, and not the nation, had been the unit of industrial and commercial relations. Now that the guild and town system of regulating industry was decaying, and the modem capitalist and competitive system was beginning its history, Elizabeth's government had to build up a national system for the regulation of industry under the direct control of the Crown. This did not mean that towns ceased to take responsibility for the welfare of their inhabitants. Much that the national government did had been tried out in towns like Norwich first, such as poor relief funded by a compulsory poor rate.

The great Statute of Artificers (or Apprentices), 1563, aimed at regulating the conditions of labour in all manufacturing industries throughout the country. It stressed the importance of agriculture

---

[32] Gill, *Studies in Midland History*.

by making it compulsory for all able-bodied men, who were not

Statute of Artificers 1563

employed in certain specified trades, to work on the land. It fixed the hours of labour (5 a.m. to 7.30 p.m. in summer, dawn to dusk in winter). It enforced the old system of seven years' apprenticeship for industrial training, which had been weakened by the decay of the guilds and by the growth of the newer individual methods of industry. Finally, the Justices of the Peace, 'calling unto them such discreet and grave persons as they shall think meet', were empowered to fix the rate of wages for all workmen in their locality, and to vary them to accord with the general level of prices.

This Labour Code for those at work was followed by a Poor Law System for those who could not or would not work. The chief motive for setting up the system was not pity for the poor, but concern for

The Elizabethan Poor Law

social order. The authorities were particularly worried about the problem of unemployed vagrants, who could easily become a terror to local populations in an age when there was no professional police force. Various statutes (1563, 1572, 1598) were passed and were made permanent in the great Poor Law Code of 1601, which remained the law of the land for two centuries and more. The impotent poor were to be maintained; pauper children apprenticed; the able-bodied unemployed found work; and the idlers placed in Houses of Correction, or workhouse prisons, and forcibly trained to work. Every parish was expected to do all this through its own officials and to meet the expense out of a poor-rate levied on all its householders. The Justices of the Peace were empowered to assess the poor-rate and to appoint Overseers of the Poor to carry out the law. The Parish and the Justice were often only the Manor and its Lord under other names. In former ages the Church had enjoined charity as a Christian duty, and the monasteries had set the example in alms-giving. Henceforth the principle was established that the state (acting through the J.Ps supervised by the Council) had a duty to provide for those who were living in destitution. Perhaps the main point of the Poor Law was to persuade the poor of the state's concern for them and so to make violent uprising less likely, for the sums expended under the Law were modest, lower, for example, than those spent by private people on relief of the destitute.

It was intended that this poor relief should apply only to those who were 'poor in very deed'. Far different was to be the treatment meted out to those rogues with whom England was 'exceedingly pestered':

> Hark, hark, the dogs do bark,
> The beggars are coming to town!

The sturdy beggar was to be brought before the Justices and, if convicted, was to be whipped and 'burnt through the gristle of the right ear with a hot iron', and sent back to his native parish. If he had no parish 'settlement', as it was long called, then the beggar was to go to a House of Correction, 'there to be employed in work until he shall be placed in some service'. If a branded person 'fall again to any kind of roguish or vagabond trade of life', he should be treated as a felon. These harsh measures were intended to rid England of what was regarded as a crying evil.

Shakespeare portrays one such rogue in Autolycus (*A Winter's Tale*), and in *King Lear* (Act II, Scene iii) he shows how the vagabonds used to terrify poor country folk. Nevertheless, this harsh law no doubt pressed on many poor wretches who were vagrants through no fault of their own; though there were few to pity them or think, as Shakespeare thought of their miserable life, in all weathers:

> Poor naked wretches, wheresoe'er you are,
> That bide the pelting of this pitiless storm,
> How shall your houseless heads and unfed sides,
> Your loop'd and window'd raggedness, defend you
> From seasons such as these?[33]

---

[33] *King Lear* (Act III Scene iv).

Conclusion

Could Henry VIII have returned from the dead in 1603, he would surely have felt keenly disappointed with the achievements of his dynasty. Far from becoming a great European dynasty, the Tudors had not even succeeded in producing heirs. Henry had no grandchildren and the throne passed therefore to the descendants of his sister. Whereas he had tried to revive the claim of English Kings to the French throne, his daughter Mary had lost even the toehold in France which the Crown still possessed, the town of Calais. England had not been swallowed by the mighty empire of Spain, but it remained a power of the second rank only. The kingdom lacked the financial or military resources of Spain or (once it recovered from nearly forty years of civil war) France. Henry's effort to re-endow the monarchy with the plunder of the Church had failed to achieve more than a temporary increase in royal wealth. For this reason Henry's expenditure on the arts at such palaces as Hampton Court and Nonsuch could not be maintained by his daughter Elizabeth. England seemed still to be a cultural backwater. Shakespeare was in time to become a playwright of international renown, but around 1600 anyone who wrote in English could scarcely acquire fame beyond the limits of the kingdom.

Yet the Tudors did leave their mark on England. They elevated the authority of the King (or Queen) acting in Parliament above that of the Church or the formerly semi-independent lords of the marches of Wales. They reduced even powerful Englishmen and Welshmen to obedience. If it was still possible for a disappointed great man like Essex to attempt rebellion in 1601, the fiasco of his rising showed that this kind of protest had no future. Popular revolt, a feature of English history since 1381, also died out in the Tudor period. Tudor governments assisted the process by enforcing a measure of social responsibility on the wealthier members of society through cajoling and bullying the JPs into implementing the Poor Law and limiting social evils such as enclosure. At the end of the 16th century the condition of the poor was probably worse than it had been at any time since the Black Death of the mid-14th century and yet the so-called Oxfordshire rising of 1596 attracted only four rebels.

Tudor England was a particularly well governed state, as a comparison with France, pulled apart by social conflicts and the rival ambitions of great families, plainly shows. Later 16th century France was also pulled apart by religion. It was perhaps Queen Elizabeth's greatest success that she managed to prevent the outbreak of religious war in her kingdom. After all the chopping and changing of the period 1530-58, Elizabeth succeeded in securing the acquiescence of most people in her religious settlement of 1559. She had not totally extinguished Catholicism, but it was reduced, except in Ireland, to the faith of a small and powerless minority. By 1603 the national religion was unquestionably Protestantism, and Catholicism had become identified for most Englishmen with burnings at the stake and with treasonable plots and threats of foreign invasion. Protestantism and patriotism had become identified. So it was that as their reigns receded into the past, the Welsh-born Tudors came to be thought of as the most quintessentially English of the royal dynasties to rule the country, in contrast to the Stuarts, initially Scottish and later linked to France and Catholicism.Acadie, see Nova Scotia.

INDEX

INDEX

INDEX

INDEX